PREFACE

The *Hobart Papers* are intended to contribute a stream of authoritative, independent and lucid analysis to the understanding and application of economics to private and government activity. Their characteristic theme has been the optimum use of scarce resources and the extent to which it can best be achieved in markets within an appropriate framework of laws and institutions or, where markets are inoperable, by other methods.

One of the main institutions has been the system of taxes designed to finance goods and services provided collectively through government. How far these activities should be confined broadly to 'public goods' (those which cannot be refused to people who refuse to pay for them) and how far government has been wise to extend its activities far beyond them is itself the subject of increasing attention by economists and is discussed in other IEA *Papers*.[1] The increasing attention by economists in the last decade to the functioning of government has produced the new theories of politics and public choice, which have located sources of 'government failure' corresponding to the 'market failure' that has pre-occupied economic writing almost since the foundations of modern economics were laid in the middle and late 18th century.

Even more recently, and especially since the accelerated inflation began in 1969-70, economists have been drawn to examine the efficiency with which government has managed the taxation required to finance its activities. There is wide agreement among economists that a structure of taxation that is not revised in a period of inflation has effects on efficiency and equity. The solution they have been examining is that of indexing tax rates, bands, allowances and so on, so that the real cost to the taxpayer and the real yield in revenue to the state is unaffected by inflation. The Institute has so far published two *Papers* on indexation: Professor Milton Friedman's *Monetary Correction* in 1974 and Messrs Jackman and Klappholz's *Taming the Tiger* in 1975. Hobart Paper 72 by Dr David Morgan, a young Australian-born economist who obtained a doctorate at the London School of Economics before going to the

---

[1] T. W. Hutchison, *Markets and the Franchise*, Occasional Paper 10, 1966; Gordon Tullock and Morris Perlman, *The Vote Motive*, Hobart Paperback 9, 1976; Ralph Harris and Arthur Seldon, *Pricing or Taxing?*, Hobart Paper 71, 1976

[3]

International Monetary Fund, is the Institute's third contribution to the subject. (He emphasises that the text was written before he took his IMF post and that it is a personal statement.)

Dr Morgan's main purpose is to examine the consequences of failing to adjust the tax system in a period of inflation. He concludes strongly in favour of indexing as the means to neutralise the effects of inflation. In an absorbing study of the subject he reveals that other Western industrialised countries in Europe, North America and Australia, where inflation has not been as severe as recently in Britain, have introduced forms of indexation; and he refutes the reasons used in other countries against it. The absentees from his list of 12 countries include the USA, Germany, Japan and France, but their governments have sinned much less in permitting inflation to envelop their economies.

For Britain Dr Morgan's analysis of the convulsive effects in distorting the tax structure of failing to index tax rates, bands and allowances requires, and repays, close study. His illustrative statistics show what may be regarded as a shocking fall in the real value of tax allowances by 30 per cent and in tax bands by 40 per cent in two years. And he says that politicians have been able to claim credit for making tax 'concessions' in terms of *money* which did not even restore the *real* value of the tax allowances and bands. Inflation is thus taxation by misrepresentation.

An aspect of the subject elaborated by Dr Morgan is that inflation gives government increased revenue from the existing tax structure for which it does not have to risk public odium by having to ask openly and candidly for public agreement to raise tax rates. Here Dr Morgan argues for automatic indexation that is taken out of political control as superior to *ad hoc* indexation at the discretion of politicians. His intriguing examination of the machinery by which revenue is raised in Britain to finance government expenditure reveals that, although the general form of decision-making in Cabinet is much the same as in other Western countries, Britain has the unique distinction of separating decisions on expenditure from decisions on tax-raising. Government in Britain, it seems, does not have a Budget but a shopping catalogue: it decides how much it would like to spend and then sets about raising the necessary money by taxation whether or not taxpayers are happy to provide the taxes. And if it cannot raise enough by

[4]

taxes it prints the money or borrows it abroad, and passes the buck to future British taxpayers to finance government expenditure—mostly not of the character of 'public goods'—that contemporary taxpayers do not want and would not willingly pay for. Indexation, Dr Morgan concludes, would make government more accountable to the public and might help to reduce the rate of extension of its expenditure.

A question raised by Dr Morgan's analysis of the lack of control over government expenditure in a period of inflation is not only whether the machinery of decision-making in Britain could be over-hauled to institute the required controls, or even whether indexation by itself will suffice. It raises the even more fundamental question, which applies to government expenditure in principle if there is inflation or not: whether government expenditure can be adequately controlled to reflect public preferences if government services that are not public goods are supplied 'free' or at much less than market prices. The question is whether a reform of the budgetary machinery and indexing must be supplemented by charging.

Dr Morgan has produced an absorbing study indicating reform in the British tax structure for which there is mounting argument and evidence. The Institute is grateful to Professor A. R. Prest and Mr Richard Jackman, both of the London School of Economics, for reading an early draft and offering comments and suggestions that Dr Morgan has borne in mind in his final revision. Its constitution requires the Institute to dissociate its Trustees, Directors and Advisers from the analyses and recommendations of its authors, but it presents Dr Morgan's *Hobart Paper* as a skilful, impressively documented and searching analysis of a means of correcting the inefficiencies and injustices of inflation. It commends itself to students and teachers of economics and to non-economists in industry, the trade unions, in public life, government, the civil service and in the communications media and elsewhere, concerned about the continuing damage to the British economy and society.

February 1977   ARTHUR SELDON

[5]

CONTENTS

[8]

GLOSSARY

AVERAGE TAX RATE—The ratio of tax liability (computed according to the tax rate schedule) to gross income.

FIRST IN, FIRST OUT (FIFO) STOCK VALUATION—Method of stock valuation whereby stocks are treated as used up in the same order as they are bought.

FREE RIDER—An individual or group who can benefit from a commodity or service produced by others without paying for it.

GROSS INCOME—The income of taxpayers computed in accordance with income tax legislation, minus deductible expenses incurred in gaining or producing it.

MARGINAL TAX RATE—Marginal tax rates are specified in income tax legislation as applying to increments to income.

PERSONAL AND DEPENDENT ALLOWANCES—Amounts specified in the tax legislation that are deductible from gross income to compute tax liability.

PROGRESSIVE TAXATION—The average tax rate rises when moving up the income scale.

REAL TAX RATES—Tax rates on ('real') incomes expressed in prices during a given base period, thereby removing the effects of changes in prices.

STRAIGHT-LINE DEPRECIATION ALLOWANCE—Provision for depreciation whereby an equal absolute amount (based on the original cost of capital equipment) is written off each year.

TAXABLE INCOME—Gross income minus dependent and non-dependent allowances deductible under the income tax legislation.

TAXABLE INCOME BANDS (OR BRACKETS)—Successive slices of taxable income taxed at increasing marginal rates.

TAX ELASTICITY—The ratio of the percentage change in tax liability to the percentage change in income.

Tax Equity: Horizontal—The principle that those in equal economic circumstances should be taxed equally.

Vertical—The principle that those in unequal economic circumstances should be taxed unequally (to what extent has remained the central issue in normative tax theory). In personal taxation the main instruments for horizontal equity are dependent allowances; and the main instrument for vertical equity, the progressive tax rate schedule.

Tax Rate Schedule—The legislated taxable income bands or brackets (i.e. successive slabs of taxable income: £1-5,000, £5,001-6,500, and so on) and the marginal tax rates that apply to each.

THE AUTHOR

David Morgan was born in 1947 and educated at Malvern Grammar, Melbourne High, and La Trobe University, Melbourne, Australia. He graduated from La Trobe University in 1970 with a Bachelor of Economics degree with First Class Honours; Economics Prize for top student. Employed as economist in the Australian Treasury in 1971 and 1972 on the balance of payments and budget research and development. Master of Science (Economics) degree with Distinction from the London School of Economics, 1973; Ely Devons prize for top student. Visiting scholar in the Fiscal Affairs Department, International Monetary Fund (IMF), Washington, DC, during the summers of 1973 and 1974. Principal researcher for the Committee of Inquiry into Inflation and Taxation established by the Australian Government in early 1975. Completed a PhD on personal tax indexation under Professor Alan R. Prest at the London School of Economics in 1976. Currently economist in the Fiscal Affairs Department of the IMF.

ACKNOWLEDGEMENTS

I would like to thank Mr Arthur Seldon and Professor Alan Tait for their helpful comments on an early draft. This *Paper* was largely completed before I joined the IMF. It presents my personal opinions and is not in any way to be interpreted as official IMF views.

November 1976   D.M.

I. INTRODUCTION

That the combination of inflation and a progressive tax system produces an increase in the real burden on taxpayers has long been recognised.[1] Until recently this process was considered to provoke no serious problems. On the contrary, it was considered desirable on economic and political grounds.

Conventionally, the tendency for tax systems automatically to generate a ('marginal') increase in total tax revenues more than proportionate to the marginal increase in total money incomes was regarded by the Keynesian school of economics as desirable, contributing powerfully to the built-in stability of the economic system.[2] Rising money incomes were a symptom of an increasing pressure of demand on available resources. Automatic tax-rate increases reduced disposable incomes in the private sector, thereby diminishing the pressure of demand. This post-war conventional view assumed that the additional tax revenue was frozen and did not stimulate additional government spending. Indeed, in 1966, the Canadian Royal Commission on Taxation, whilst emphasising that real rather than nominal (money) income was the appropriate base for income taxation, said that any attempt to adjust taxes automatically for the effects of inflation would 'irreparably damage' the built-in stability of the economic system.[3] Politically, the combination of inflation and progressive taxation allowed governments to increase the real tax burden painlessly, without having to bear the voters' displeasure for explicitly increasing tax rates by new legislation. Alternatively, they could gain kudos by announcing a tax 'cut' that in effect was nothing of the kind but merely maintained the real burden of tax.

1. The end of fiscal illusion

During the past decade, an increasing number of countries has introduced schemes to neutralise this supposedly desirable relationship between inflation and progressive personal taxation. Two obvious reasons for this development were the

[1] Jacob Viner, 'Taxation and Changes in Price Levels', *Journal of Political Economy*, August 1923.

[2] Richard A. Musgrave, *The Theory of Public Finance*, McGraw-Hill, New York, 1959, pp. 510-512.

[3] *Report of the Royal Commission on Taxation*, Queen's Printer, Ottawa, 1966, Volume 2, p. 23. Canada has since introduced personal tax indexation (IV below).

[13]

accelerating rate of inflation and the weight of personal taxation. They increased the importance of the relationship, and undermined the fiscal illusion of taxpayers that unchanged *money* tax rates during inflation implied stable *real* tax burdens.[1]

This increased public awareness not only reduced the political attractiveness of the relationship; it also sparked off reactions that tended to exacerbate both inflation and unemployment—mainly from trade unions in the form of 'wage retaliation' against higher taxation, which developed into bargaining over 'take-home' pay that ignored the 'social wage'. This new trend was evident in Britain,[2] Canada,[3] Sweden, Austria and Ireland.[4] Shifting increases in personal income tax from the employee to employer and/or consumer is likely not only to exacerbate inflation and unemployment, but also to reduce the efficacy of personal taxation as an instrument for counter-inflation policy, for transferring resources to the government sector, and for redistributing income within the private sector.

2. The newly-discovered time-lag between real output and inflation

Post-war experience in developed economies also reduced the economic attractiveness of the relationship between inflation and taxation for built-in stability through macro-economic demand management. One important assumption of the conventional post-war view of the stabilising power of personal taxation during inflation was that there was a close relationship

[1] The OECD contend that such increased awareness became apparent in most developed economies between 1968 and 1970. (Kenneth Messere, 'The Impact of Inflation on Tax Structures', in *Inflation, Economic Growth and Taxation*, Institut International de Finances Publiques, Barcelona, 1975.)

[2] Dudley Jackson, H. A. Turner and Frank Wilkinson, *Do Trade Unions Cause Inflation?*, Cambridge University Press, 1972. Further supporting empirical evidence may be found in J. Johnston and M. Timbrell, 'Empirical Tests of a Bargaining Theory of Wage Rate Determination', *Manchester School of Economic and Social Studies*, June 1973, and in S. G. B. Henry, M. C. Sawyer and P. Smith, 'Models of Inflation in the United Kingdom: An Evaluation', *National Institute Economic Review*, August 1976. These and other aspects are also discussed in three IEA Readings: Gottfried Haberler, Michael Parkin and Henry Smith, *Inflation and the Unions*, Readings No. 6, 1972; Lord Robbins *et al.*, *Inflation: Economy and Society*, Readings No. 8, 1972; Milton Friedman *et al.*, *Inflation: Causes, Consequences, Cures*, Readings No. 14, 1974.

[3] C. J. Bruce, 'The Wage-Tax Spiral: Canada 1953-1970', *Economic Journal*, June 1975.

[4] Thomas F. Dernburg, 'The Macroeconomic Implications of Wage Retaliation Against Higher Taxation', *International Monetary Fund Staff Papers*, November 1974.

between the time-paths of real output and inflation. There is now a huge body of empirical evidence refuting this assumption. In developed economies, a change in total demand tends to produce a *prompt* effect on real output while the effect on wages and prices tends to be *delayed*.[1] These lags would not be particularly important if they were fully recognised, and acted upon, by policy-makers. But the evidence is that they are not:

'. . . policy makers may sometimes have been misled by accepting a mistaken diagnosis . . . confusion has on occasion been caused by identifying wage and price movements with *current* demand pressures. Wages and prices in industrialised countries respond strongly to rapid rises in output and employment, but effects take some time to become evident and may persist for 12-18 months after the rise in output has slowed down. Failure to appreciate this caused a number of countries to hesitate . . . to take adequate action against the recession, because wages and prices were continuing to increase.'[2] [My italics.]

Given the time-lags and the political failure to act on them, the effect of price changes on tax revenue is itself potentially destabilising, because tax revenue increases rapidly in response to an inflation which reflects *past* demand pressures, at a time when real output is falling in response to *current* slack in demand. The trouble is that the real value of taxes will continue to increase as long as *money income* is rising, not as long as *excess demand* persists.[3] Therefore the conventional consensus that the desirable automatic stabilising properties of the personal tax system ought to be preserved can no longer be taken for granted.

3. Revenue-induced government spending

Contemporary experience has also called into question a second assumption of the conventional wisdom: that additional

---

[1] A lag of at least one year of the price cycle behind the real output cycle was confirmed for OECD countries from 1956 to 1966. (*The Growth of Output 1960-80*, OECD, Paris, 1970, Appendix VII.) These results are consistent with the evidence from full-scale macro-econometric models: for example, the results of the simulations for the Bank of Canada's RDX2 model in *The Structure of RDX2—Part 1*, Bank of Canada, Ottawa, 1971, pp. 250-252.

[2] *Fiscal Policy for A Balanced Economy*, OECD, Paris, 1968, p. 86.

[3] If employment declines sharply and the rate of wage and price increase is relatively moderate, total money incomes may decline. This outcome does not vitiate the basic argument above that the delayed response in wages and prices impairs the automatic stabilising effect conventionally attributed to a progressive tax system.

tax revenues thrown up by the combination of inflation and progressive taxation are frozen and do not stimulate additional government expenditure. It has usually been argued that, for developed economies (unlike developing economies), tax policy tends to accept the amount of government expenditures as its goal for raising revenue. The sequence of decision has been regarded as running from government expenditures to taxes.[1] But an authoritative study of fiscal policy in several developed economies from 1955 to 1965 revealed a widespread *opposite* tendency towards a 'natural budget reaction': a tendency for governments to spend whatever revenues happened to be collected.[2]

Given the lag of price movements behind changes in real output, it may seem that a tendency for governments to spend inflation-induced tax revenues would be an appropriate instrument of stabilisation policy. But these unlegislated transfers of resources to the government sector have not been accepted passively by the private sector. In 1972 the OECD drew attention to

'. . . the process by which resistance to attempts to shift the distribution of expenditure away from 'pure' [i.e. privately financed] private consumption generates inflationary pressures'.[3]

By 1974 they concluded:

'The available evidence suggests that in Member countries the change in the rate of inflation has been greatest in those countries where the growth rate in the share of public expenditure has been most rapid'.[4,5]

[1] W. H. Heller, 'Fiscal Policies for Underdeveloped Economies', in Richard M. Bird and Oliver Oldman (eds.), *Readings on Taxation in Developing Countries*, Johns Hopkins Press, Baltimore, 1967, p. 10. A contrary view, with particular attention to the role of inflation and personal taxation, is in Alan T. Peacock and Jack Wiseman, *The Growth of Public Expenditure in the United Kingdom*, Allen and Unwin, London, 2nd Edition (revised), 1967, p. 32.

[2] Bent Hansen, *Fiscal Policy in Seven Countries 1955-1965*, OECD, Paris, 1968, p. 61. Professor Milton Friedman has long argued that government expenditures are tax-determined rather than *vice-versa*: e.g. in *Inflation: Causes, Consequences, Cures*, IEA Readings No. 14, *op. cit.*, p. 76.

[3] *Expenditure Trends in OECD Countries 1960-1980*, OECD, Paris, 1972, p. 47.

[4] *Economic Survey of Australia*, OECD, Paris, 1974, p. 37.

[5] [Dr Colin Clark has recently refined his theorem (*Economic Journal*, 1945), broadly approved by J. M. Keynes, on the relationship between inflationary pressures and the proportion of taxes to national income: *The State of Taxation*, Readings No. 16, IEA, 1977.—ED.]

4. *Reappraisal of the taxation-inflation relationship*

Accelerating inflation, the increasing weight of personal taxation, the lag of changes in price behind changes in real output, the emergence of wage bargaining based on take-home pay, and revenue-induced government spending have all cast doubt on the desirability of leaving unchecked the interaction of inflation and progressive taxation. More and more countries have introduced schemes to neutralise their personal tax systems against inflation. The aim of this *Hobart Paper* is to consider the effects of inflation on personal taxation in Britain and, in particular, to examine the case for neutralising this part of the British tax system against them by indexing.

Section II briefly reviews the impact of inflation on the size and composition of government revenues and expenditures *in toto*, and considers the implications of inflation for the distribution of the personal tax burden between (real) income groups, family sizes, and income sources (wage and salary income, investment income, and capital gains). Section III discusses the objectives of personal tax indexation, and compares the schemes proposed to achieve them. Overseas experience with indexation is surveyed briefly in Section IV. Section V proposes a scheme appropriate to British conditions, and examines the implications for tax equity, the tax mix, government expenditure and macro-economic stability. Finally, conclusions for policy are set out in Section VI.

II. THE EFFECTS OF INFLATION

Summary

With conventional fiscal systems, it is probable inflation will generate a larger increase in tax revenue than in government expenditure. However, the likelihood and the desirability of this result are challenged by contemporary experience. The second part of this section examines the mechanisms through which inflation plus unchanged personal taxes redistribute the tax burden. While high-income groups are hard hit, low-income taxpayers with large families are shown to be among those most seriously affected.

[17]

A. On Government Finances

Inflation has important consequences for the size and composition of government revenues and expenditures that can differ markedly according to the fiscal system and the type of inflation. The response of government economic policy is also important in the extent to which potential consequences eventuate. The following analysis assumes:

(i) the personal tax schedule is progressive, and personal taxation is collected under a withholding system such as 'Pay as You Earn' (PAYE);

(ii) for corporation taxes, that stocks are valued by the first-in first-out (FIFO) method, and depreciation provisions calculated as a 'straight-line' allowance based on the original cost of fixed assets;*

(iii) an *ad valorem* sales tax and excise duties in the form of a fixed money amount per unit of quantity;

(iv) inflation is generated domestically rather than imported, and does not erode the real value of aggregate personal income or alter the size distribution of personal income.

1. *The size and mix of taxation*[1]

Inflation with unchanged money tax rates is likely to change the relative contribution of the major forms of taxation to total revenue and possibly also the ratio of total revenue to Gross Domestic Product (GDP).

(*a*) *Personal taxation*

The interplay of inflation and unchanged personal taxes will result in higher average tax rates for *all* personal taxpayers; and some individuals initially exempt will be dragged into the tax net. Because the average tax rate increases continuously with money income, the ratio of personal taxes to total income will rise.

(*b*) *Other taxes*

A straight line depreciation allowance based on historical cost provides an annual deduction from corporate gross income for purposes of calculating taxable corporation income fixed in

---

* Glossary.

[1] The impact of inflation on the real rate of return on cash balances is discussed in Richard Jackman and Kurt Klappholz, *Taming the Tiger*, Hobart Paper 63, IEA, 1975, pp. 19 and 23.

money terms. Inflation erodes the real value of this deduction and, *ceteris paribus*, will increase the taxable income measured at constant prices as compared with what it would have been in a period of price stability. The same result obtains when the corporate cost-of-goods-sold calculation employs the FIFO method* of stock valuation.[1]

If the money value of excise duties remains unchanged during inflation, their real value declines. The likely, but not necessary, result is that the real value of total excise duty revenue will decline. The result is not unavoidable since a decrease in the real value of the duty may reduce the relative price of the commodity, thereby increasing its consumption. Nevertheless the result is likely because the demand for commodities commonly subject to excise duty (alcoholic beverages, tobacco, and gasoline) is not normally price elastic, so that demand will not rise appreciably.

During inflation *ad valorem* sales tax revenues probably increase automatically with inflation, assuming that prices of goods and services subject to tax rise with the general rate of inflation. The personal tax system should, however, not be ignored in considering the response of sales (and excise) tax revenues to inflation. The combination of inflation and unchanged taxation will tend to reduce disposable incomes and therefore consumption, which comprise the base for sales (and excise) taxation. So the proportionate response of sales tax revenues may be somewhat below the rate of inflation.

Inflation will tend to increase the yield of capital gains taxation where the gains are calculated simply as the difference between money purchase and selling prices, regardless of the intervening rate of inflation. Clearly a taxpayer who buys and sells an asset whose price no more than keeps pace with the rate of inflation will have to pay tax on an illusory capital gain. The tax on capital *gains* becomes a tax on *capital* itself, the rate of tax varying with the rate of inflation.[2]

(*c*) *Inflation and the tax mix*
What are the conclusions for the effects of inflation on taxation? Even if there were no changes in tax legislation during a

* Glossary.

[1] Numerical examples are in the *Report of the Committee on Company Accounts and Inflation* (Sandilands Report), Cmnd. 6225, HMSO, 1975, pp. 78-80.

[2] Similarly with the taxation of investment income during inflation.

[19]

sustained inflation, no *a priori* conclusions could be drawn about the likely impact of inflation on the ratio of total taxation to GDP because tax revenues depend, *inter alia,* on whether an income tax is levied at proportional or progressive rates, and whether a consumption tax is levied at *ad valorem* or specific rates. We should have to know the initial relative weights of each type of taxation, and, in particular, of progressive compared with specific taxes. But the likely conclusion is that, *ceteris paribus,* the relative weight of progressive taxes would increase and the relative weight of specific taxes would decrease. Given the type of tax structure assumed here, this conclusion implies that the weight of taxation on income would increase compared with that on expenditure.

Table I sets out the percentages of total receipts from taxes on income, expenditure and capital in Britain from 1964 to 1975. The main feature is the increasing contribution of taxes on income relative to those on expenditure: 52·1 per cent of tax revenue in 1975 as compared with 42·6 per cent in 1964; conversely, taxes on expenditure yielded 53·7 per cent in 1964 and 45·2 per cent in 1975.

Many factors have produced this pattern, but it is significant that, in the period of relatively moderate inflation from 1964 to 1969, the rise in the share of taxes on income was also extremely modest. It was after 1969, when inflation began to accelerate, that the share of income taxes began to increase markedly, especially since the very high inflation from 1973. Inflation has been an extremely important contributing factor, since discretionary personal tax changes in recent years have been nothing like sufficient to offset the effects of inflation fully (below).

(d) Implications of increased personal taxation
What are the implications of such a trend? First, expenditure taxation tends to be more encouraging to saving than income taxation, since income taxation reduces the *net* rate of interest, thus lowering the rate at which individuals can substitute future for present consumption.[1] Secondly, arguments in favour of a 'balanced' tax structure may be supported on the grounds that large and rapid changes in the tax 'mix' require adjustments by economic agents (labour changing jobs,

[1] Some caveats to this proposition may be found in A. R. Prest, 'The Expenditure Tax and Saving', *Economic Journal,* September 1959.

TABLE I

COMPOSITION OF TAX RECEIPTS: BRITAIN, 1964-1975

	Taxes on Income[a]	Percentage Share of Total Taxation *Taxes on Expenditure*[b]	*Taxes on Capital*[c]
	%	%	%
1964	42·6	53·7	3·7
1965	43·4	53·5	3·1
1966	43·5	53·4	3·1
1967	44·5	52·5	3·0
1968	43·7	52·9	3·4
1969	43·0	52·8	4·2
1970	44·9	51·0	4·1
1971	45·7	50·5	3·8
1972	44·7	51·1	4·2
1973	45·5	50·4	4·1
1974	49·9	46·6	3·5
1975	52·1	45·2	2·7

(a) Central government receipts, principally of income tax and corporation tax.

(b) Central government receipts of indirect taxes plus local authority rate income.

(c) Central government receipts of taxes on capital gains and death duties.

Source: Government Statistical Service, *Economic Trends Annual Supplement 1975*, HMSO, 1975, and *Economic Trends*, August 1976.

investors switching investments, etc.) that are not costless. Thirdly, there may be significant increases in administrative costs for the tax-gatherers because increased personal taxation usually introduces a large number of new taxpayers at very low incomes.

(e) *Tax avoidance and evasion*

Finally, it is relevant to discuss here possible public reaction against the increasing rates of income taxation that are predominant features of the change in the tax 'mix' induced by inflation. As marginal rates of tax increase, so also do the rewards from tax avoidance. There may be substantial, although inconspicuous, economic waste in altering investment and employment decisions to avoid higher income taxes.

Investments are likely to be favoured whose pre-tax yield is lower than that of others, but whose after-tax yield is higher. There may be a shift of employment into industries, occupations or areas where non-monetary rewards are highest (less smoke, dirt, noise, danger, as well as tax-free fringe benefits).[1] There may be a more general shift towards activities attracting income in kind rather than money income, like do-it-yourself activities (home, garden, car) rather than earning taxed income and paying for services with what is left in the pay-packet. There may be more barter: the painter may pay the dentist with a painting, and the bricklayer and plumber help each other to build houses; no-one knows how far barter is used to avoid tax, least of all the Inland Revenue, because it is not recorded.

The search for ways to minimise liability to tax will affect the amount the government has to spend identifying the tax loopholes thus opened and closing them without opening others. A vicious circle can develop whereby frustrated legislators step up marginal tax rates, thereby further increasing rewards from, and thus themselves stimulating, avoidance (as well as hastening the move to the ultimate tax-deterrent—avoidance by emigration).[2] When a small amount of tax avoidance is worth a very large increase in income, the resulting waste of resources on both sides may be substantial. Everyone loses—except tax consultants.

Increased avoidance may also lead to increased evasion. Avoiders graduate to evasion, perhaps when some loopholes are closed. The example of avoidance inspires others to try evasion, perhaps because they cannot use avoidance. While the distinction between avoidance and evasion is legal rather than economic, evasion is perhaps more serious since it is harder to identify and more difficult to cure. Also, the cures themselves may be of a nature that hastens the decline of taxpayer morality. The lower the willingness of the public to

[1] In his 1976-77 Budget speech, the Chancellor noted that Britain has far more of these fringe benefits than comparable countries. (*Hansard*, Vol. 909, No. 85, column 276.)

[2] The Chairman of the Board of Inland Revenue testified recently: 'I think avoidance is growing and in my view it has become a national habit'. (*First Report From the Expenditure Committee*, HMSO, 1975, p. 182.) In other testimony, the Inland Revenue openly described tax evasion in Britain today as 'very serious indeed'. (*Local Government Finance: Report of the Committee of Enquiry* (Layfield Report), Cmnd. 6453, Appendix 8: 'Local Income Tax: Evidence and Commissioned Work', HMSO, 1976.)

accept that the tax system (including its enforcement) is 'fair' and equitable, the more severe evasion becomes.

The relationship between tax rates and avoidance and evasion, moreover, may be non-reversible. Rising tax rates are likely to induce increased avoidance and evasion, but subsequent tax-rate reduction will not necessarily eliminate the new habits and practices. Like the loss of innocence, avoidance and evasion are probably irreversible.

2. *Government expenditure*

The Chancellor of the Exchequer has argued that inflation caused the budget deficit to grow in 1974-75:

> '. . . when inflation is running at rates hitherto regarded as normal, it has little significant effect on the balance between public expenditure and receipts. But in the conditions of last year, the inflation caused by excessively large wage and salary increases raised public expenditure in money terms much more than public sector receipts, and the public sector deficit rose sharply.'[1]

If the Chancellor's argument was correct, it would cast serious doubt on the contention that governments tend to accept inflation because it improves their *net* revenue, and therefore that tax indexation was politically undesirable. The Chancellor's argument appears to be invalid both in the context of 1974-75 (Appendix A) and more generally for fiscal systems similar to Britain's.

(*a*) *Government sector productivity*

In analysing changes in the 'price' of government expenditures, it is important to distinguish between growth in real and money income. Measured growth in productivity is less in the government than in the private sector. In part, this is because it is usually possible to observe only government sector inputs (cost of materials, labour, etc.) but not outputs (value to consumers, beneficiaries).[2] In any event it is still likely that growth in government sector productivity would be lower because it is generally highly labour-intensive. (Given that wages in the two sectors tend to move with each other, the

[1] Budget Speech, *Hansard*, 15 April 1975, column 279.

[2] A frequent convention used for national accounting is that output at constant prices per government employee is constant through time.

[23]

'prices' of government goods will tend to increase more rapidly than the prices of private goods[1] because of lower rates of growth in productivity rather than inflation *per se*.)

(b) Current expenditure on goods and services

To what extent is inflation likely to generate automatically an increase in government expenditures proportionately less than, equal to, or more than the automatic response of revenue? On the current expenditure side, the prices of goods bought by government are likely to increase with inflation. Government wages and salaries can also be expected to increase with their private sector counterparts, and hence keep up with inflation. Incomes policies may bear more heavily on government wages and salaries, but it seems doubtful that they will permanently change differentials between the two sectors. Recent British experience would appear to support this supposition:

> 'Some special settlements made in the public sector were intended to correct anomalies that developed from the operation of the statutory [incomes] policy.'[2]

(c) Capital expenditures

There is no strong reason for supposing that government capital expenditures would fail to increase with inflation. It is by no means certain that inflation will raise the price of labour relative to that of capital. The cost of any finished good or service, no matter the capital-labour ratio, can resolve itself (in a closed economy) into only two sources of costs: personal payments to labour and to capitalists; it can thus ultimately be decomposed into labour costs and interest charges. As long as labour costs and interest charges are adjusted similarly to inflation, the relative price of labour to capital will, *ceteris*

---

[1] The presentation of public expenditure projections in Britain includes an adjustment for what is termed the 'relative price' effect, which embodies two elements: to take account of the differential price movements in the cost of the inputs to the public sector, and to try to correct for the understatement of public sector productivity inherent in the assumption that the change in the value of public sector output at constant prices is proportional to numbers employed. (P. M. Rees and F. P. Thompson, 'The Relative Price Effect in Public Expenditure: Its Nature and Method of Calculation', *Statistical News*, HMSO, August 1972.)

[2] *Financial Statement and Budget Report 1975-76*, HMSO, 1975, p. 5.

paribus, remain unchanged.[1] Hence, capital expenditures would tend to move in line with inflation.

(d) Debt interest

If the rate of inflation is stable, and the average rate of interest on central government debt has been adjusted to it, government interest payments will increase with inflation only to the extent that the government maintains the real value of its outstanding debt. If inflation accelerates, government interest payments are likely to rise less rapidly than inflation, the shortfall being determined by the turnover of existing debt, the average interest rate on it, and on new borrowing. But, to the extent that the central government is operating as an intermediary for lower layers of government or for public corporations, account must be taken of the likelihood that central government interest receipts will also increase less than inflation.

(e) Transfer payments

A recent survey revealed that indexation of government (state, as distinct from occupational civil service) pensions was widespread among developed economies,[2] but less so for other social security payments (unemployment benefits, family allowances, and income supplement payments).[3] Some of them may be inversely related to the money income of recipients. Hence if the money income qualifying limits are not raised with inflation, these payments may shrink in money terms. The extent to which central government grants to lower layers

---

[1] A rigorous exposition of this argument is in Paul A. Samuelson, 'A New Theorem on Nonsubstitution', in Joseph E. Stiglitz (ed.), *The Collected Scientific Papers of Paul A. Samuelson*, Massachusetts Institute of Technology Press, 1966, Vol. I, pp. 520-536. Also E. J. Mishan, 'Payroll Taxes Promote the Use of Labour-Saving Machinery', in *Twenty-One Popular Economic Fallacies*, Penguin, London, 1969, pp. 44-51.

[2] S. A. B. Page and Sandra Trollope, 'An International Survey of Indexing and Its Effects', *National Institute Economic Review*, November 1974. Countries indexing pensions included Belgium, Canada, Denmark, Finland, France, Netherlands, New Zealand, Norway, Britain, and the United States. The survey did not include West Germany, and did not show Sweden as indexing pensions, though it appears that both do so. See Santosh Mukherjee and Claire Orlans, *Indexation in an Inflationary Economy*, PEP Broadsheet No. 551, London, 1975, p. 15.

[3] This does not imply necessarily, of course, that these payments will fail to keep pace with inflation.

[25]

of government and other institutions keep pace with inflation will no doubt vary according to the institutional conditions.[1]

(f) Subsidies

Government subsidies can be appreciably affected by inflation.[2] Farm price support payments may fall as inflation moves food prices towards the stipulated target fixed in money terms. Clearly, precisely the opposite effect on government expenditures can occur with rent or food subsidies, or payments to public corporations, aimed at maintaining fixed prices to the consumer. Such open-ended commitments will involve continually increasing payments from the government as long as inflation continues. Other types of subsidy, such as cheap credit to the private sector and tax concessions ('tax expenditures'), can grow substantially in value during inflation, although conventional accounting methods may not record any increase in government assistance.

(g) Government policy during inflation

The implicit assumption so far has been that inflation *per se* has no direct impact on the volume of government expenditure. But it creates uncertainty among the public, if not alarm or even fear. They see inflation as outside their control and naturally press government to control costs imposed by inflation, real or imagined. Further, there will be a natural desire by government to be seen to be contributing actively towards a solution.

Unfortunately, government frequently resorts to policies that exacerbate the trouble. Politicians have been unable (or unwilling) to grasp a crucial distinction, long emphasised by economists, between, first, required adjustments in some *relative* prices that may change the equilibrium price (*average*) 'level', and, second, inflation of *all* prices, relative prices possibly remaining unchanged, which is a dynamic disequilibrium characterised by an excessive growth in the money supply. The policy that would go to the root cause of

---

[1] In Australia, for example, grants from the central government to the States are automatically increased with inflation. In the US, no such adjustment is made. The British practice (before April 1976) of grants to local authorities calculated as a fixed percentage of their expenditures implied that these grants would automatically keep pace with inflation.

[2] Following Professor Prest, a subsidy is defined as a government payment that directly affects relative prices in the private sector. (*How Much Subsidy?*, Research Monograph 32, Institute of Economic Affairs, 1974.)

the problem, reduction in the money supply, is, for the politician, frequently too slow and inconspicuous. Governments characteristically prefer policies such as food subsidies to private producers and/or fuel subsidies to state corporations that the public (or they themselves) see as having a direct and quick effect on the measured price *level*, but are 'cosmetic' because they have no effect on the underlying *rate* of inflation. Indeed, they usually exacerbate it, as their cost induces government to generate further monetary expansion. Thus, inflation *per se* does not expand the volume of government expenditure but rather encourages policies that are ultimately self-defeating.

(h) Cash limits or 'funny money'?
Inflation *per se* can lead to a fall in the volume of government expenditure if, during the budget year, it is faster than anticipated at the start of the year, and government expenditures have fixed cash limits. If government expenditure is 'planned' in *real* terms (so-called 'funny money'), inflation, anticipated or unanticipated, is unlikely to change its volume. For the US it has been argued that the former prevails, at least for non-wage expenditures, and hence real government expenditures are reduced by inflation.[1] In Britain, on the other hand, government expenditure is planned almost exclusively in real terms.[2] It is generally agreed that, apart from an influence on subsidies, inflation did not play a major role in the large increase in real government expenditures in Britain from 1970-71 to 1974-75.[3]

3. *Implications for macro-economic stability*
Given a relatively modest role for specific taxes in the fiscal structure, and the absence of substantially increased tax avoidance and evasion during inflation, total tax receipts

---

[1] Edward M. Gramlich, 'Measures of the Aggregate Demand Impact of the Federal Budget', in Wilfred Lewis, Jr. (ed.), *Budget Concepts for Economic Analysis*, The Brookings Institution, Washington DC, 1968.

[2] The cash limits introduced in the 1976-77 Budget are discussed in Appendix B.

[3] For instance, the discussions between the UK Expenditure Committee and Treasury and Bank of England officials in *First Report from the Expenditure Committee*, HMSO, December 1975. With local authorities able to make their own evaluation of price increases, it is possible that some real expenditure increases took place under the guise of adjustment for inflation. (*Ibid.*, Vol. II, paras. 782 and 889.)

would change more than a purely money change in income (for the type of tax structure assumed above). It would seem reasonable to conclude that, in the absence of large open-ended subsidies, government expenditures are unlikely to rise by more than the rate of inflation. The application of weights to items of the budget that change in real terms as a result of inflation, reflecting the impact of the change on demand for domestic resources, would not seem to alter the general conclusion that a 'neutral' government economic stance during inflationary periods constitutes a more restrictive fiscal policy than it does in times of price stability.

Conventionally, the role of taxation and inflation in producing such a result was regarded as desirable, contributing to the built-in stability of the economic system. But this role is trebly challenged by contemporary experience:

- increasing money incomes do *not* necessarily indicate a state of generalised excess demand throughout the economy;
- increased tax rates may *not* restrain disposable incomes because trade unions respond to the increased taxes by using their power to induce governments to inflate; and
- it *cannot* be assumed automatically that the additional tax revenue will be 'frozen'.

These issues are considered in Section V.

B. On the Distribution of the Personal Tax Burden

What are the mechanisms through which inflation plus unchanged personal taxes redistribute the tax burden? What are the effects on the equity objectives of the personal tax system?

1. *The mechanisms of tax burden redistribution*

A major misconception concerning the relationship between inflation and progressive taxation is that a taxpayer needs to be moved into a higher tax bracket to be affected adversely. Given the wide first taxable income bracket* in Britain (currently from £1 to £5,000) it may be thought that only higher-income groups (with taxable incomes in excess of £5,000) suffer from an unindexed tax schedule. Certainly

* Glossary.

high-income groups are hard hit, but low-income taxpayers with large families are among those most seriously affected.

There are two basic mechanisms by which tax is redistributed, deriving from the relationship between taxable and gross income and between tax liability and taxable income.*

(a) Taxable and gross income

The relationship between taxable and gross income is determined by the form and size of allowances. Where they are fixed in money amounts, inflation will result in taxable income increasing more rapidly than gross income. The proportion of gross income subject to tax will therefore increase, even though *real* gross income is unchanged, thus increasing average tax rates for all taxpayers initially subject to personal taxation (and for some initially exempt) even with a proportional tax rate. The rate of increase in taxable income for any given rate of increase in gross income varies *inversely* with the initial gross income.

How does the rate of growth of taxable income vary between taxpayers with the same real gross income, say the single taxpayer and the married taxpayer with dependent spouse? Since the allowance for a married taxpayer exceeds that for a single taxpayer (in Britain as well as generally), the rate of increase in taxable income will be higher for the married taxpayer. The same conclusions hold for taxpayers with more dependants. The higher the total of dependent allowances, the larger the proportionate increase in taxable income *vis-à-vis* a taxpayer with smaller dependent allowances at the same initial gross income. Hence low-income taxpayers with large families will tend to have the largest proportionate increase in taxable income (Table III).

(b) Tax liability and taxable income

The second mechanism of tax redistribution is found in the progressive tax rate.* Except in the first taxable income bracket, any increase in taxable income generates a proportionately larger increase in tax liability. All of the increased taxable income faces a marginal tax rate at least as high as the top marginal rate faced by the pre-inflation taxable income. Hence, with inflation, a larger proportion of any real taxable income

* Glossary.

[29]

will become subject to the higher marginal tax rates. The outcome is an increase in the real tax liability associated with each real taxable income.

(c) Inflation and tax rates

If all gross incomes simply match the rate of inflation, the combination of the two mechanisms (a) and (b) usually results in the largest proportionate increase in tax liabilities, and hence the largest proportionate increase in average rates of tax, falling on the lowest real gross incomes. These differing proportionate increases imply a redistribution of the personal tax burden between real gross incomes. There will also be a redistribution of the tax burden between taxpayers according to numbers of children, the large family taxpayer being most adversely affected (Table III).

These results are not dependent on the assumption that gross money incomes increase with the rate of inflation. For instance, assume instead that money incomes are not adjusted at all to the rate of inflation. Clearly, taxpayers' average tax rates will remain unchanged. But the average tax rate on every level of real income, for every group of taxpayers, has increased because the real gross income of every taxpayer has declined yet each taxpayer continues to be taxed at the same average rate that applied when real incomes were higher.

(d) Contrasts with real income growth

These conclusions should be contrasted with real income growth. The important difference between 'real' and inflationary income growth is that when the increase in income reflects real growth, no redistribution of the tax burden between real incomes takes place. Unlike the case where purely money income increases occur, real incomes just below relevant allowance limits, for instance, will continue to be exempt from personal taxation. This result holds for all real income levels and for all taxpayer categories and hence there is no redistribution of the tax burden between real income levels or taxpayer categories.

(e) Equity implications

For horizontal and vertical equity,* proportionate changes in average tax rates would seem to provide the most appropriate criteria for measuring the redistribution of the tax burden

* Glossary.

caused by inflation and progressive taxation. If the implications for wage bargaining were to be examined, it might be more appropriate to examine changes in real take-home pay arising from unchanged personal taxes during an inflationary period. Indeed, from the point of view of stabilisation policy generally, and the allocation of real resources between the government and private sectors, changes in real take-home pay would seem to be more appropriate criteria than proportionate increases in average tax rates.

With progressive taxes, an increase in gross money income just equal to the rate of inflation results in an increase in money take-home pay less than the rate of inflation. Hence, real take-home pay will decline. Again, the rate of decline varies between real gross incomes in a quite complex manner. The usual tendency with progressive tax schedules is for the proportionate decline to vary directly with real gross income; the higher gross incomes tend to suffer the larger declines.

However, *within* any taxable income band, the decline in real take-home pay is larger the *lower* the income. This result assumes considerable importance in Britain, where the incomes of the vast majority of personal taxpayers fall within the first £1 to £5,000 taxable band. The combination of inflation and unchanged taxes in the range where most taxpayers fall is therefore adverse to lower-income taxpayers according to the criteria both of proportionate increases in tax rates *and* proportionate declines in real take-home pay. Table II shows the proportionate increase in tax liabilities and average tax rates, and the proportionate decrease in real take-home pay, for real gross income groups under the 1975-76 British income tax schedule, assuming a rate of inflation of 20 per cent in 1975-76.[1] Table III compares the tax rate increases and reductions in real take-home pay borne by married taxpayers with two and four dependent children. It confirms that the large family taxpayer is almost invariably affected more adversely than either the small family taxpayer or the single taxpayer (Table II).

2. *Discretionary adjustments and inflation*

When the analysis is extended beyond a single year, it is

---

[1] The rate of inflation in 1975-76 (April over April) as measured by the Index of Retail Prices was 18·9 per cent.

TABLE II

PROPORTIONATE INCREASE IN TAX LIABILITIES
AND AVERAGE TAX RATES AND PROPORTIONATE
REDUCTION IN REAL TAKE-HOME PAY: SELECTED
REAL GROSS INCOME LEVELS OF THE SINGLE
TAXPAYER, 1975-76 RATE SCALE

Real Gross Income £	Proportionate Increase in Tax Liability %	Proportionate Increase in Average Tax Rate %	Proportionate Decrease in Real Take-Home Pay %
1,500	36·4	11·4	3·3
2,000	30·2	10·8	2·6
2,500	27·4	6·2	2·1
3,000	25·8	4·8	1·8
3,500	24·8	4·0	1·6
4,000	24·1	3·4	1·4
4,500	24·4	3·6	1·5
5,000	26·9	5·8	2·5
6,000	29·5	7·9	3·7
8,000	31·9	11·0	5·6
10,000	31·1	10·9	6·4
15,000	29·9	8·3	8·1
20,000	29·4	7·8	9·8
50,000	24·3	3·6	6·6

Note: Assumes 20 per cent rate of inflation in 1975-76; no deductions from gross
income other than the personal allowance.

Source: Calculated from *Financial Statement and Budget Report 1975-76*, HMSO,
London, 1975.

possible to examine the extent to which discretionary adjustments to allowances and band limits have kept pace with
inflation. The base period for the comparisons is April 1973,
when the unified rate scale was introduced to replace the
surtax system.

(*a*) *Decline in real value of dependent allowances*

Table IV and the Chart show the decline in the real value of
the personal and dependent allowances since April 1973. By
the close of the 1975-76 financial year, the *real* values of
allowances were, on average, only 70 per cent of their originally
legislated values, despite increases in their *money* values in the

TABLE III

COMPARISON OF TAX RATE INCREASES AND REAL TAKE-HOME PAY REDUCTIONS FOR MARRIED TAXPAYERS WITH DEPENDENT CHILDREN, 1975-76 RATE SCALE

	Percentage Increase in Average Tax Rate Married Taxpayer		Percentage Decrease in Real Take-home Pay Married Taxpayer	
Real Gross Income £	*With Two Dependent Children* %	*With Four Dependent Children* %	*With Two Dependent Children* %	*With Four Dependent Children* %
2,000	37·3	121·4	4·5	5·7
2,500	20·7	39·4	3·8	4·8
3,000	14·2	23·4	3·3	4·2
3,500	10·9	16·7	2·9	3·7
4,000	8·8	13·3	2·6	3·3
4,500	7·4	10·8	2·4	3·0
5,000	6·8	8·8	2·3	2·7
6,000	10·1	10·9	3·7	3·7
8,000	12·0	13·3	5·6	5·8
10,000	11·5	12·9	6·6	7·2
15,000	9·6	10·4	8·2	9·1
20,000	8·6	9·1	9·7	10·6
50,000	2·9	3·1	7·0	7·7

Note: The calculations assume that all income is earned, that the dependent children are under eleven, and that income includes family allowances. 'Clawback' has been taken into account at all levels of income. Other assumptions are as for Table II.

Source: As for Table II.

budgets of 1974-75 and 1975-76.[1]

Assuming an inflation rate for 1976-77 of 12·8 per cent,[2] the *real* value of allowances by the close of that financial year would on average be only 75 per cent of their originally legislated values, despite the seemingly large *money* increases granted after the 1976-77 budget.

(b) Decline in real width of taxable income bands

The decline in the real width of taxable income bands is even

[1] The child allowances were not increased in the 1975-76 Budget.

[2] This inflation rate is derived on the basis of the actual rate of inflation to August 1976, and an assumed rate of 1 per cent per month until March 1977.

TABLE IV

DECLINE IN REAL VALUE OF ALLOWANCES, APRIL 1973 TO MARCH 1977 (ESTIMATED)
(£: APRIL 1973 = 100·0)

Real Value as at:

Allowance	April 1973	March 1976[a]	March 1977[b]
	£	£	£
Single allowance	595	413	398
Married allowance	775	584	588
Child allowance			
Not over 11	200	147	163
11-16	235	168	182
Over 16	265	186	198

(a) Calculated on the basis of the values of the allowances for 1975-76, deflated by the Index of Retail Prices.
(b) Calculated on the basis of the 1976-77 allowances, deflated by the Index of Retail Prices assuming an inflation rate of 12·8 per cent in 1976-77.

TABLE V

REAL VALUE OF UPPER LIMIT OF TAXABLE INCOME BANDS

April 1973	March 1976[a]	March 1977[a]
£	£	£
5,000	2,751[b]	2,711[c]
6,000	3,668	3,524[c]
7,000	4,280	4,066[c]
8,000	4,891	4,609[c]
10,000	6,114	5,422
12,000	7,336	6,506
15,000	9,170	8,133
20,000	12,227	10,844

(a) Deflation procedure and 1976-77 inflation assumptions as for Table IV.
(b) Includes the effect of the discretionary decrease in the upper limit in the 1974-75 budget.
(c) Includes the effect of the discretionary increase in the upper limits announced in the 1976-77 budget.

more striking (Table V), since there have been hardly any discretionary changes since April 1973.[1] At the end of 1975-76, the real widths of almost all taxable income bands were only 60 per cent of their originally legislated widths. The real width

---

[1] In the 1974-75 budget, the upper-income limit of the first band was decreased from £5,000 to £4,500. It was restored to £5,000 in the 1976-77 budget when the upper-income limits of the next three bands were increased by £500 also.

PERSONAL INCOME TAX: DECLINE IN REAL VALUE OF PERSONAL AND DEPENDENT ALLOWANCES, APRIL 1973 TO MARCH 1977

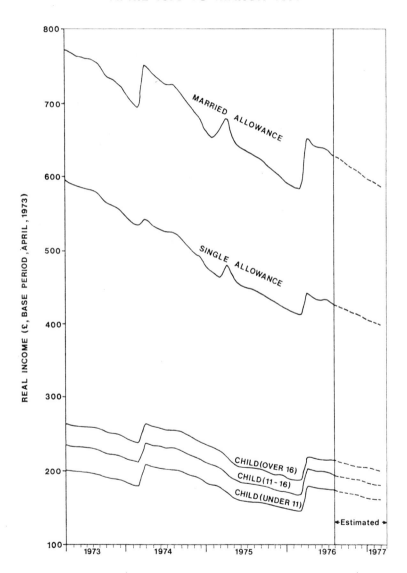

of the first taxable income band was almost halved, the additional shrinkage being due to a downward discretionary adjustment in the 1974-75 budget. By the close of the 1976-77 fiscal year, the real widths are projected to decline further to just over half their originally legislated values.

3. *Non-wage and -salary income*

Inflation creates exceptional difficulties for the taxation of investment income and capital gains. The basic difficulty is essentially the same: inclusion in the tax base of income that merely compensates for the erosion in the real value of the investment.

Assume prices are stable with a 5 per cent interest rate. A taxpayer with savings of £1,000, subject to a marginal tax rate of 50 per cent, will be left with an after-tax real rate of return of 2·5 per cent. If inflation is running at 10 per cent and the monetary rate of interest is 15·5 per cent (having adjusted itself fully to the rate of inflation), his after-tax return is insufficient to compensate him for the erosion in the real value of his capital, implying a negative real rate of return. The tax on interest *income* becomes a tax on the *capital*.[1]

With capital gains, a taxpayer who buys and sells an asset whose price does nothing more than keep pace with the rate of inflation, so that he has not increased his command over real goods and services, will have to pay tax on a *fictitious* capital gain. Equally clearly, the basic fault lies in the faulty definition of the tax base.

4. *Tax burden redistribution and tax equity*

Several studies have examined the effects of inflation on the distribution of the personal tax burden and confirmed the general pattern analysed here. One on Canada concluded:

'. . . inflation is a clumsy way of raising taxes, with surprising and unintended effects on burden distribution.'[2]

The Canadian Finance Minister described these effects as 'unfair and unintended'.[3] For Britain, R. I. G. Allen and

---

[1] Vito Tanzi, 'Inflation, Indexation, and Interest Income Taxation', *Banca Nazionale Del Lavoro,* March 1976.

[2] George Vukelich, 'The Effect of Inflation on Real Tax Rates', *Canadian Tax Journal,* July-August 1972, p. 342.

[3] The Hon. John N. Turner, *House of Commons Debates,* Budget Speech, 19 February 1973, p. 1,434.

D. Savage (both then on the research staff of the NIESR) found:

'It is clearly difficult to argue that this pattern of redistribution reflects anything but a haphazard and inequitable approach to social policy.'[1]

In whatever manner the equity intentions of the personal tax schedule are described at the time of legislation, they will be distorted by inflation. It may be argued, even if cynically, that failure on the part of governments to adjust taxes for inflation is itself a 'discretionary' adjustment, and therefore presumably reflects the preferences of society in the distribution of the personal tax burden. This argument implies not only that public preferences change during inflationary periods, but also that the changes wrought by inflation are those preferred by the public. Given the arbitrary nature of the inflation-induced tax redistributions, it would be fortuitous if they corresponded exactly with government intentions or public preferences.

It also assumes that political representatives reflect public preferences accurately. Public retaliation against inflation-induced tax increases ('take-home' pay bargaining, increased tax avoidance and evasion) implies either that politicians are unaware of the effects of leaving tax schedules unchanged during inflation, or that they are aware but do not wish to reflect public preferences.

III. OBJECTIVES AND METHODS OF INDEXATION

The most common method adopted by governments to meet the problems raised in Section II has been to adjust, from time to time, the major deductions and allowances defined in money terms, and make *ad hoc*, discretionary, decreases in tax rates and/or increases in taxable income bands. In recent years, however, more countries have introduced more *automatic* adjustment of allowances and bands by indexation. What are its objectives and methods?

[1] R. I. G. Allen and D. Savage, 'The Case for Inflation-proofing the Personal Income Tax', *British Tax Review*, No. 5, 1974, p. 302.

1. *The objectives*

Equity is the main *rationale*. The legislated schedule of tax rates and allowances aims to provide an equitable distribution of the burden between taxpayers according to real income, size of family, and so on. Inflation and unchanged taxes significantly alter the distribution of the burden between taxpayers, thereby violating the equity expressed in the schedule. Indexation aims to neutralise this effect of inflation.

That these equity judgements are of central importance to the tax system would not seem in dispute. The Australian Taxation Review Committee comments:

'. . . establishing the "right" degree of progressivity by reference to the criterion of equity is . . . fundamental to tax policy . . .'.[1]

The quotation emphasises progressivity as the way to achieve tax equity, as well as the central importance of the equity objective itself.

The Committee dramatises an aspect crucial to an understanding of the objectives of indexation:

'The central and sensitive question here [concerning the appropriate degree of progressivity] is that of the *relativity* of one individual's tax bill to another's. In analysing this issue it is unavoidable to proceed by comparing the total taxes they pay, but the argument is properly about the *differences* between the totals rather than about the totals themselves.'[2] [My italics.]

That is, progressivity and therefore equity are concerned with *relative* rather than absolute tax burdens. The interplay of inflation and progressive taxation generates an increase in the tax burden that is distributed in a manner inconsistent with the legislated objectives of equity. Indexation aims to maintain *relative* tax burdens between real incomes and taxpayer categories. The most obvious method of maintaining these relativities is to adjust the allowances and bands with the rate of inflation to restore the legislated average tax rates on each real gross income group. If it is estimated that the aggregate revenues forthcoming will be inconsistent with the government's macro-economic expenditure or stabilisation requirements, a proportional across-the-board tax levy might bring the required result:

[1] *Full Report of the Taxation Review Committee,* Australian Government Publishing Service, Canberra, 1975, para. 3. 18.

[2] *Ibid.,* para. 4. 3.

'If stabilisation and equity objectives are to be reconciled, two policy instruments will be needed, including (1) an index adjustment to raise bracket limits, and (2) an across the board increase in tax rates, sufficient to more than offset the revenue loss from (1).'[1]

Indexation does not imply that relative tax burdens legislated in a base year are sacrosanct and inviolable. It takes any legislated tax structure and maintains its relative burdens until explicitly altered by government. It does not, in intent or effect, tie the government to a fixed distribution of the tax burden for all time. On the contrary, it provides government with more, rather than less, control over the distribution. It is true that indexation implies that government must *explicitly justify* any departure from the original distribution. Yet the relatively short history of indexation in practice indicates that governments do not regard it as constraining their freedom to make significant discretionary adjustments.

2. *The methods*

There are three methods of indexation.

(a) *Allowance and band adjustment*

The most common is to widen bands and allowances. The increase in allowances maintains their real value so that the same proportion of any given real gross income is exempted from tax as in the absence of inflation. Similarly, taxable income band adjustment maintains their real width and ensures that the same proportion of any given real taxable income will face each marginal tax rate as in the absence of inflation. Assuming no change in marginal tax rates, the two adjustments taken together ensure the maintenance of the initial average tax rates.

This result emerges independently of the response of money incomes to inflation. If a taxpayer's money gross income increases faster than inflation, his real gross income has, of course, increased, and so too will his average tax rate under the adjustment scheme. Similarly, if his real gross income declines, so too will his average tax rate, to the level specified in the legislated tax schedule.

---

[1] Richard Musgrave, 'Tax Structure, Inflation and Growth', in *Inflation, Economic Growth and Taxation, op. cit.*, p. 13.

(b) Gross income adjustment

A second form of indexation adjusts income for inflation, leaving the tax schedule unchanged. Money gross income is expressed in terms of base year prices, and taxable income and tax liability are calculated in terms of the base year tax schedule. The tax liability so calculated is then converted into current prices. Reflation of tax liabilities calculated in terms of the base year tax schedule is necessary so that the real value of personal tax liabilities is maintained.

(c) Adjustment according to changes in money income

In a third scheme, bands and allowances are adjusted with the rate of increase in per capita money incomes.[1] As discussed above (sub-section (b)), the redistributive effects of inflation on tax burdens persisted whatever the response of money incomes to inflation. These redistributive effects are offset by conventional indexation regardless of the response of money incomes. An obvious and important difference between conventional indexation and adjustment according to changes in money income is that the latter provides adjustment for inflation *only to the extent that money incomes are adjusted fully and rapidly to the rate of inflation*.

Where money incomes rise faster than the rate of inflation, adjustment according to changes in money incomes will mean that increases in real income are automatically accompanied by decreases in tax rates; and again a redistribution of the tax burden will ensue, in an opposite direction to the position in Section II. To the extent that real incomes increase continuously over time, real tax rates will, of course, continuously decline. The primary objective of such adjustment would seem to be to maintain the initial overall *size* of the aggregate tax burden, rather than the initial *distribution*. On the assumption that the pre-tax distribution of personal income does not change significantly, adjustment according to changes in per capita money income will result in the aggregate tax ratio remaining constant through time (assuming also, of course, that no other significant tax changes accompany the adjustment). Constancy of the aggregate tax ratio is not an

---

[1] Vito Tanzi, 'A Proposal for a Dynamically Self-Adjusting Personal Income Tax', *Public Finance*, No. 4, 1966. Professor Tanzi suggests changes in either the nominal personal income/population ratio, or the nominal GNP/population ratio as the index to be used for adjustment.

objective of indexation based on the rate of inflation. Movements in the aggregate tax ratio are properly determined by reference to government expenditure and stabilisation requirements. Adjustment for the effects of inflation is a separate issue.

3. *Exemption of cost-of-living increments*

During the post-war period up to 1975, Israel exempted cost-of-living increments from taxation. Assuming that all money gross incomes are adjusted fully to inflation, the initial distribution of the tax burden is restored. This result is not achieved by restoring the initial average tax rates, for real tax rates would then decline because taxpayers' incomes have been reckoned in real terms but not their tax liabilities. Such a procedure is equivalent to an income deflation scheme where tax liabilities calculated in terms of the base year tax schedule are not revalued at current prices. Conventional indexation does not exempt cost-of-living increments from personal taxation. The effect is to tax cost-of-living increments at a marginal tax rate equal to the average rate.

If money incomes are not adjusted at all to inflation, the adjustment scheme clearly disappears. If money incomes are adjusted only partially, the adjustment will only partially offset the redistributive effects. Adjustment for the effects of inflation is forthcoming only to the extent that income earners obtain full compensation for inflation. One of the advantages of conventional indexation is that it provides some tax relief for taxpayers whose real gross incomes decline during inflation, and they are likely to be in the weaker bargaining positions. Clearly such adjustment is likely to have discriminatory effects. It is therefore not obvious that it will be successful in achieving the equity objectives of indexation.

4. *Indexation of non-wage and -salary income*

If the money interest rate is adjusted fully to the rate of inflation, recipients of interest income would, before tax, maintain the real value of their income and of their financial asset (Section II). Under conventional indexation, the income that merely compensates for the reduction in the real value of the asset would be treated as an increment to real income and taxed at the relevant marginal rate. This fault is not properly attributable to indexation *per se* but to a definition of taxable income that fails to allow for the inflation-induced reduction in the real value of the monetary asset. The most straightforward solution is to exclude this component from taxable income, lenders deducting from their taxable income a figure equal to the outstanding principal amount of the debt multiplied by the rate of inflation.[1] This procedure does not depend upon the money interest rate being adjusted fully to inflation. The rate of inflation multiplied by the principal amount of the debt appropriately measures the inflation-induced reduction in the real value of the asset, regardless of the response to inflation of the money interest rate.

With capital gains, the cost base of the asset should be written up to represent the current money equivalent, and tax levied on the excess over the sale price. The price index should reflect general prices, rather than the price of capital assets, otherwise it would eliminate genuine gains (or losses) resulting from an increase (or decrease) in the relative price of capital assets.

IV. OVERSEAS EXPERIENCE WITH INDEXATION

The most common indexation schemes overseas adjust bands and allowances. Of the 12 countries in this short survey, seven have introduced indexation since the accelerated inflation of the past decade. Two have traditionally experienced high rates of inflation.

A. COUNTRIES

1. *Denmark*

In 1969 Denmark introduced indexation by providing that allowances and bands be adjusted with changes in the consumer price index, less the price effects of indirect taxes and government subsidies. Since 1975, Denmark has operated a scheme similar to that proposed by Professor Tanzi, where allowances and bands are increased with the increase of average wages. The scheme differs from adjustment according to changes in money incomes since the average wages calculated are of the work force in employment. Thus, given a

---

[1] Similarly, borrowers would be required to add to their taxable income a figure equal to the amount borrowed multiplied by the rate of inflation.

rapid increase in real wages, any associated decline in employment will not be reflected directly in average wages. Hence, where there is a contraction in the personal tax base (due to the decrease in employment) indexation based on average wages may result in a large decline in real tax rates (due to adjustment on the basis of average wages). This outcome may be considered desirable for macro-economic stabilisation, but the likely implications for personal tax revenues are difficult to ignore.

Conventional tax indexation, it has been claimed, may assist in moderating wage claims. It is difficult to see such a benefit flowing from indexation based on movements in average wages, because the larger the increase in average wages relative to the rate of inflation the larger the decline in real tax rates *vis-à-vis* the legislated rates. It will be recalled that, under conventional indexation, real taxes will never fall below the legislated rates, regardless of the rate of wage increase, or the inflation that may flow from such an increase.

2. *Netherlands*

Indexation in the Netherlands dates from 1972. The consumer price index used for adjustment excluded changes in indirect taxes and government subsidies. The factor used for correction in 1972 and 1973 could be less than the change in the consumer price index by a maximum of 20 per cent. Indexation was suspended for 1974. It was reactivated in 1975, with no downward adjustment to the correction factor.

3. *Luxembourg*

Formal provisions for automatic indexation of allowances and bands were introduced in Luxembourg in 1967. Explicit adjustments for inflation were made in 1965 and 1966. The legislation stipulated that bands and allowances for the following tax year be adjusted whenever the consumer price index for the first six months of the current tax year rose by at least 5 per cent over the corresponding period for the previous year. Had Luxembourg adhered strictly to this formula, only one adjustment would have been forthcoming between 1968 and 1974. In the event, four adjustments were made. Thus, the 5 per cent inflation threshold provision has not proved as costly to the taxpayer as the legislation implies.

[43]

4. Canada

In 1973 Canada introduced indexation from the start of the 1974 tax year. Bands and major allowances were adjusted for inflation on the basis of a consumer price index unadjusted for indirect taxes or subsidies. The implied lag between the inflation rate used in calculating the adjustment and the rate of inflation during the tax year is 15 months. Indexing is asymmetric: if the price level declines there will be no downward adjustment of bands and allowances.

5. Switzerland

Four Swiss Cantons empower the authorities to make adjustments for inflation. They vary between the Cantons, as does the degree to which they have been implemented. The record reveals a pattern of *ad hoc* discretionary changes rather than automatic indexation.

6. Chile

In 1954 Chile introduced indexation with exemptions, allowances and bands defined in basic salaries. Clearly, the efficacy of the indexation turns on the extent to which they keep pace with inflation.

7. Brazil

In 1961 Brazil introduced a similar scheme. Personal exemptions and bands were fixed as multiples of the minimum wage, which was changed by decree each year fairly closely with the rate of inflation; hence the exemptions and bands were automatically adjusted for inflation. During 1964, the real value of the minimum wage declined, resulting in increased tax burdens for all real incomes. In November, exemptions and bands were defined in conventional monetary units instead of multiples of the minimum wage.

8. Uruguay

In 1967 provision was made for adjustment of the personal exemption and dependent allowances in line with inflation. This provision ensured adjustment of the tax bands as well, since they were expressed as multiples of the personal exemption.

9. Argentina

In 1972 Argentina introduced indexation covering exemptions and deductions, but not bands.

[44]

10. Iceland

In 1966 deductions and bands were made adjustable (upwards or downwards) each year in accordance with a tax index. The basis for calculation of the index was not indicated, although

'. . . movements [in the index] . . . take into consideration changes in prices and real incomes'.[1]

11. Israel

The post-war tax legislation to 1975 provided that the inflationary component of wage and salary increases could, at the discretion of the Minister of Finance, be exempted from personal taxation. The deficiencies of such a scheme have been noted in Section II.

To what extent could the Israeli indexation be viewed as part of an incomes policy? Conventional indexation is sometimes regarded as an undertaking by the government not to increase real tax rates in return for moderation by trade unions in negotiating increases in money wages.[2] It is difficult to place the Israeli scheme within this category. To the extent that unions were prepared to forego full adjustment of money wages to inflation, they were foregoing the maximum downward adjustment of real tax rates. To obtain personal tax relief, it was necessary to have a cost-of-living increment; and the larger the increment, the more the reduction in real tax rates. To the extent that indexation is considered an important ingredient of incomes policies, the Israeli model would not appear to be ideal. In 1975 the scheme was replaced by the conventional adjustment of tax bands and allowances in line with inflation.

12. Australia

In 1976 the Government announced proposals for indexation, to be applied to all tax bands and dependent allowances, and to the main non-dependent allowances with fixed upper-income limits. Indexation was to be based on the average annual increase in the Consumer Price Index, adjusted to remove the price effects of discretionary changes in indirect taxes. The first adjustment was made in 1976 at 13 per cent.

---

[1] *Economic Survey of Iceland,* OECD, Paris, December 1974, p. 21.

[2] Lars Matthiessen, 'Index-Tied Income Taxes and Economic Policy', *Swedish Journal of Economics,* March 1973, p. 62.

[45]

B. Why have Countries Indexed?

Countries adjusting bands and allowances according to an index of incomes rather than prices (Denmark and Iceland) have done so in response to rapid increases in the relative size of their government sectors and to pressures to curtail them. In countries adjusting according to an index of prices, the Latin American schemes are clearly a response to rapid rates of inflation. In Australia, the initial pressure for indexation came from the trade unions, stimulated by the rapid inflation of 1973-74. The Labour Government instituted an inquiry in 1975, but felt unable to accept the Committee's strong recommendation in favour of indexation in the 1975 Budget because of the extremely strong growth of government expenditures. The Liberal Government of 1976 introduced indexation to produce 'a desirable discipline upon future Government spending decisions',[1] emphasised in the Treasurer's Budget Speech:

> 'This brake upon financial profligacy is a major step towards "keeping governments honest" with their taxpayers.'[2]

In the remaining countries, no common factor emerges. They did not experience exceptionally rapid inflation or increases in personal tax liabilities before the introduction of the schemes, nor were absolute personal tax liabilities particularly high relative to comparable economies.

C. Why have Countries not Indexed?

Some countries, notably West Germany, Sweden and Finland, have displayed particular hostility towards indexing.[3] They have argued that it deals with the *results* of inflation, rather than its *causes*, and would therefore weaken governmental and public resolve to stop it. They also fear that indexing one component of the economic system would encourage economy-wide indexation. These (and other) objections are considered in Section V.

---

[1] Australian Treasurer, *Fiscal Policy Decisions*, 20 May 1976, p. 7.

[2] *1976-77 Budget Speech*, AGPS, Canberra, August 1976, p. 28.

[3] Germany requires persons who wish to enter into indexed contracts to obtain permission from the central bank. In Finland, since 1969, indexation has been illegal except for pensions, insurance and some long-term contracts.

V. PERSONAL TAX INDEXATION FOR BRITAIN

A. The Proposal

This section outlines a scheme that is equitable to the taxpayer, administratively feasible, and easily integrated with existing budgetary procedures.

1. *The form and scope of indexation*

Adjustment of bands and allowances would seem better than deflation of gross income. It would be more easily understood, and administratively less costly because no change in existing procedures is required.[1] It would also tend to be more consistent with additional discretionary tax changes, since income deflation requires reference back to a base year tax schedule.

The scheme should apply to all bands and to the personal and all dependent allowances. It should also include the inflation adjustments for capital gains and investment income (Section II). The interest income taxable in lenders' hands should be that deductible by borrowers, and *vice-versa*. If inflation adjustment is applied to interest income for personal tax purposes, the same adjustment should therefore also be made for corporate taxation. The Sandilands Committee made no such recommendation for corporate taxation, in part because of this implication for personal taxation which they took to be beyond their terms of reference.[2]

2. *Choice of a price index*

A recent *Hobart Paper* argued that the price index of Gross Domestic Product at factor cost was better for generalised indexation than the Index of Retail Prices.[3] The authors argued correctly that, for indexing *money incomes*, it is crucial to distinguish between *generalised* inflation and *relative* price changes occasioned by indirect tax increases or by a deterioration in the terms of trade. For tax indexation, however, the

---

[1] There may be some administrative saving under a gross income deflation because new tax tables would not have to be issued each year, assuming the absence of discretionary tax adjustments accompanying indexation. Income deflation and tax reflation 'factors' would need to be issued to employers to calculate the tax withheld, thereby increasing compliance costs.

[2] *Op. cit.*, para. 689.

[3] Richard Jackman and Kurt Klappholz, *Taming the Tiger*, Hobart Paper 63, IEA, 1975.

change in the *real* purchasing power of the pound in the hands of the taxpayer is best measured by the unadjusted Index of Retail Prices.[1]

All countries that adjust bands and allowances automatically measure inflation by an index of consumer prices, although some (Netherlands, Australia) exclude the price effects of discretionary changes in indirect taxation. It is argued that indirect tax changes are aimed at securing a transfer of resources between the private and government sectors, and indexation based on an unadjusted price index will offset part of it. If this argument for removing the effects of indirect tax changes from the price index is valid, it is not clear why it should be confined to indirect taxation and not applied also to changes in company taxation, for example. The logical extension of the argument is that the component of total inflation that comes about as a result of government policies designed to shift resources from the private to the government sector should not be included in the index. This would include not only price movements attributable to changes in all forms of taxation, but also any price increases generated by increased government borrowing, or by increases in the money supply generated to finance budget deficits. *All* policies aimed at shifting resources from the private to the government sector have potentially inflationary implications. It seems arbitrary to single out indirect taxation.

Another argument is that the appropriate measure of real income is not the taxpayer's command over private goods and services but also over those supplied by government. If this view is accepted the whole issue of tax rates becomes unimportant. It would not matter how tax rates were levied, or changed, since a taxpayer's real income would remain unaltered even if his tax rate doubled overnight or consumed all his income. All that would alter is the mix of government and privately supplied goods and services at the command of the taxpayer, i.e. the mix of his private wage and 'social' wage.[2]

The objection to this argument is that the incidence of all the benefits of government expenditures cannot be ascertained

---

[1] A detailed discussion of the appropriate price index (supporting the above measure) is in *Report of the Committee of Inquiry into Inflation and Taxation*, Australian Government Publishing Service, Canberra, 1975, pp. 165-184.

[2] 'Social' wages and their relevance to indexation are discussed in sub-section B.5(*d*) below.

by any known techniques. Even a demonstration that people who suffered the largest increase in their tax burden (as a result of removing indirect tax effects from the index) received the most benefit from increased government expenditures would not justify such removal. For it supposes that those who enjoy the most benefits should bear the largest tax burdens. Progressive taxes explicitly reject such an approach.

3. Conclusions

Within a climate of relatively moderate and stable inflation, a single adjustment of bands and allowances at the time of the annual budget would adequately satisfy the equity objectives of indexation. At a minimum, adjustment should be applied to the personal allowance, dependent allowances, and all taxable income bands. The rate of increase in the allowances and bands should be equal to the rate of inflation as measured by the average rate of increase in the Index of Retail Prices over the previous calendar year.

B. Implications of Indexation

1. Equity implications

The combination of inflation and unchanged allowances and bands will redistribute the tax burden between real incomes, family sizes, and income sources (Section II). These redistributions violate legislated equity prescriptions, both horizontal and vertical,* which would be maintained by indexation. Real income provides a better measure of capacity to pay than money income. Equity considerations constitute the major *rationale* for indexation.

(a) An indexed 1976-77 tax schedule

How would the British 1976-77 tax schedule look if indexation had been introduced with the unified rate scale in April 1973? Dependent allowances would have been as shown in Table VI. The indexed values in the left-hand column are *minima*, since they make no allowance for erosion by inflation in 1976-77. The values indicate only the real income equivalent at April 1976 of the allowances introduced in April 1973. The indexed

*Glossary.

TABLE VI

INDEXED AND ACTUAL ALLOWANCE VALUES, 1976-77

| | Indexed Value | | |
| | With no Adjustment for 1976-77 Inflation | With Adjustment for 1976-77 Inflation | Actual Allowances for 1976-77 |
	£	£	£
Single allowance	992	1,041	735
Married allowance	1,292	1,356	1,085
Child allowance			
Under 11	333	350	300
11-16	392	411	335
Over 16	442	464	365

values in the middle column incorporate such an adjustment.[1] The allowances for 1976-77 are substantially below (on average 25 per cent) those that would have maintained the original real values. Under an indexed system, a married taxpayer with two children would be exempt from tax in 1976-77 if his gross income was below £2,230. The exemption limit without indexing is 20 per cent lower, at £1,785.

The discrepancy between taxable income bands in 1976-77 and those that would maintain the original real widths is even more striking (Table VII). For the upper limits of taxable income bands, unchanged since the rate scale was unified, the indexed values are 75 per cent above the current values: in short, *the real widths of these taxable income bands have been almost halved.* For upper limits that have been adjusted,[2] the indexed values are more than 60 per cent above the current values. Under the indexed system, a taxpayer with real taxable income of £5,000 in April 1973 prices would be facing a marginal tax rate of 35 per cent in 1976-77. *Under the existing unindexed system he bears a marginal rate of 60 per cent.* Such is taxation without legislation.

[1] The adjustment is based on the average increase in prices in 1976-77 as a whole over April 1976. Thus, while the assumed increase of prices between April 1976 and April 1977 is 12·8 per cent, the required increase in allowances for the year as a whole is less than half this percentage.

[2] The second, third, and fourth taxable income bands.

TABLE VII
INDEXED AND ACTUAL TAXABLE INCOME BANDS, 1976-77

Indexed Bands[a] (£)	Current Actual Bands (£)
1— 8,750	1— 5,000
8,751—10,500	5,001— 6,500
10,501—12,250	6,501— 7,500
12,251—14,000	7,501— 8,500
14,001—17,500	8,501—10,000
17,501—21,000	10,001—12,000
21,001—26,250	12,001—15,000
26,250—35,000	15,001—20,000
Over 35,000	Over 20,000

(a) Includes the adjustment for 1976-77 inflation described above, based on April 1973 values.

(b) More indirect taxation?

Some have argued that indexation would necessarily require higher indirect taxation. It is frequently alleged that indirect taxation is intrinsically inequitable, and that any shift towards it will necessarily reduce the equity of the system as a whole. That argument is not compelling.

First, indexation does not necessarily reduce tax revenues. It simply ensures that increases in the real tax burden are legislated explicitly.

Secondly, the proposition that income taxation is more equitable than indirect taxation is related to the relative balance between the two:

> 'A rational Government will always use first the means of finance that involve the lowest marginal social costs...When this first tax reaches a certain level of revenues, however, the marginal social costs of its further use may begin to exceed those of another. This is where the first tax reaches its capacity.'[1]

Given a particular balance between personal and indirect taxation it may be that, for equity, personal taxation is the appropriate instrument with which to increase the total tax burden. Obviously, this conclusion need not necessarily hold for different times or tax balances. Recent British experience

[1] Amotz Morag, *On Taxes and Inflation*, Random House, New York, 1965, p. 8.

[51]

of increased personal tax avoidance and evasion and of wage retaliation against higher taxation suggests that the marginal costs (in faster inflation and lower output) of further increases in personal taxation could be very high.

Thirdly, to the extent that increases in indirect taxation were judged necessary, the equity implications should not be considered in isolation from the rest of the taxation system or from the pattern of government expenditure.

(c) A substitute for tax reform?

A further argument is that indexation is likely to be at the expense of more fundamental and urgent tax reforms, which can be implemented only where the tax burden is, in general, reduced; and since indexation also implies a general reduction in tax burdens, the two types of reform are, in reality, substitutes. Recent experience in Canada, Australia and Israel does not support the argument that taxes can be reformed only when they are reduced. Further, many equity intentions of a reformed tax system will be rapidly and substantially distorted if indexation does not accompany reform, and if inflation continues at anything like current rates. Tax reform and indexation are thus best viewed as complementary.

(d) Must indexation be all or nothing?

A final equity objection to indexation may be that personal tax indexation in isolation compensates only one group for inflation. It may therefore increase the inequities in the redistributive effects of inflation. The argument is not persuasive:

(i) Very little empirical evidence has accompanied the much discussed cruel income redistribution effects of inflation. And the small amount of empirical research carried out for developed economies indicates that the effects of inflation *per se* on the *pre-tax* distribution of income are exceedingly modest.

(ii) Economic theory is consistent with these empirical findings. It suggests that the institutional mechanisms of a society based on freedom of choice and competition will, if it is reasonably flexible and inflation not too erratic, eliminate major inflationary injustices. Genuine economic costs of inflation, therefore, are those that cannot or will not be eliminated by competitive contract adjustments.

[52]

Over-taxation by Inflation
DAVID R. MORGAN

1. In Britain inflation has been accompanied by inadequate adjustments in tax allowances and bands so that real rates of taxation have increased sharply.

2. This inadequate adjustment is inequitable as between tax-payers, and tends to bear more harshly on low-income and large families than on higher-income and smaller families.

3. Incomplete adjustment transfers more revenue to government than taxpayers know or wish to pay. Between 1973-74 and 1975-76, personal taxes more than doubled.

4. These sharp increases in tax rates have occurred while politicians have appeared to make concessions to taxpayers by altering allowances and bands in *money* terms that do not even restore, still less enlarge, their *real* value to tax-payers.

5. Inflation is taxation by misrepresentation. Large increases in tax revenue induced by inflation exonerate politicians from asking the electorate explicitly for higher tax rates.

6. The lack of indexation has permitted government in Britain to continue its practice of separating decisions on expenditure from decisions on tax-raising. It is unique among Western industrialised countries, where the two are normally considered together in budgeting, and has contributed to a bloated public sector.

7. Increasing resistance to unlegislated increases in tax rates has emerged in Britain, in the form of wage bargaining on take-home pay and increased tax avoidance and evasion.

8. An increasing number of countries in Europe, as well as Canada and Australia, have introduced various forms of tax indexation in the last five or ten years, despite less rapid inflation than in Britain.

9. Tax indexation would make the government more accountable to the electorate and tend to limit the expansion in government expenditure, as the electorate became more aware of the tax- 'cost' of expanding government services.

10. Tax indexation could help to moderate inflation, since government would lose its major incentive to acquiesce in inflation, and wage- and salary-earners would require lower increases in gross wages to reach given targets in take-home pay.

Hobart Paper 72 is published (price £1.50) by

 THE INSTITUTE OF ECONOMIC AFFAIRS
2 Lord North Street, Westminster
London SW1P 3LB   Telephone: 01-799 3745

IEA PUBLICATIONS

Subscription Service

An annual subscription to the IEA ensures that all regular publications are sent without further charge immediately on publication—representing a substantial saving.

The cost (including postage) to subscribers in Britain is £10·00 for twelve months (£9·50 by Banker's Order). A reduction to £7·50 is made for teachers and students who pay *personally.* The overseas subscription is US $30, or the equivalent in other currencies.

To: The Treasurer,
     Institute of Economic Affairs,
     2 Lord North Street,
     Westminster,
     London SW1P 3LB

Please register an individual subscription of £10·00 (£7·50 for teachers and students who pay *personally*) for the twelve months beginning.................................

☐   Remittance enclosed   ☐ Please send invoice

☐   I should prefer to pay by Banker's Order which reduces the subscription to £9·50.

Name ....

Address ....

          ....

Position ....

Signed ....

Date..

HP72

(iii) Even to the extent that research found significant redistributions during inflationary periods, not all of them could necessarily be deemed inequitable.

(iv) Even if substantial redistributions occurred and were clearly inequitable, they may not be particularly remediable by government action.

Now consider the relevance of these four findings for the impact of inflation on personal taxation:

(i) The redistributive effects *are* demonstrably substantial.

(ii) They *cannot* be eliminated by competitive contract adjustment.

(iii) They *are* demonstrably inequitable.

(iv) They *can* be eliminated by government action—indeed, this is virtually the only form of action that can appropriately offset the redistributions.

Unchanged progressive taxation may thus produce the major inequitable redistributive effect of inflation that can be substantially offset by indexation. It seems inconceivable that failure to index personal taxes provides a more equitable economic system than with an indexed personal tax structure. Valid objections to indexation must lie in its economic and social implications other than those directly relating to equity.

2. *Implications for the tax mix*

Indexation would mean that increases in real rates of personal taxation would no longer be produced automatically by inflation, but would have to be legislated explicitly. By itself, however, it cannot be expected to halt the trend to an increasing relative role for taxes on income. Within a growing British economy, indexed taxes would be likely to remain the most elastic source of revenue available to government, since increments to real income would still be taxed progressively.

3. *Implications for government expenditure*

Indexation is likely to improve the efficiency of decision-making in government expenditure. If taxes are not indexed the relative ease of securing additional revenue may weaken the determination of government to rein in its expenditure. It may thus obscure the decision, which is in effect being made *implicitly*, to allocate more funds to government. Under indexation, additions to government expenditure demanding revenues exceeding those produced by growth in real income would require government to ask Parliament or the electorate *explicitly* for tax increases. This public request would clearly identify the effects on taxes of increased government spending. New government expenditure projects and/or existing commitments would then be subject to closer parliamentary and public scrutiny. The efficiency of government decision-making would thus improve because there would be more accountability to the taxpayer.

These arguments raise fundamental questions. How much scope is there for significant improvement in the efficiency of government decision-making? Are the tax consequences of increased government expenditure insufficiently appreciated by government and the public?

(a) The efficiency of the government expenditure decision-making process

Studies of government expenditure in several countries suggest that most Western political and administrative systems tend to expand; old activities rarely die off completely, and new ones are continually introduced.[1] There is a consistent upward trend of government expenditure beyond the amount 'required' by expansion of the population. In Britain, according to a 'Social Democrat' who was in Parliament for 10 years (1966 to 1976):

> '. . . it has become clear during the last ten years that the pattern of public expenditure is determined, not by conscious choice on the part of the society whose needs that expenditure is supposed to satisfy, and not even by the conscious choice of the elected representatives of that society, but by a haphazard combination of *ad hoc* political pressure, departmental log-rolling and bureaucratic inertia.'[2]

To understand the reasons for this deterioration it is necessary to examine how government decides how much to spend.

---

[1] For example, Richard Bird, *The Growth of Government Spending in Canada*, Canadian Tax Foundation, Toronto, 1972; and *Review of the Continuing Expenditure Policies of the Previous Government*, Australian Government Publishing Service, Canberra, 1973.

[2] David Marquand, 'A Social Democratic View', in *The Dilemmas of Government Expenditure*, IEA Readings No. 15, Institute of Economic Affairs, 1976, p. 68. Mr Marquand resigned his seat in the House of Commons in 1977 to become Political Adviser to Mr Roy Jenkins, President of the EEC Commission.

(b) *The bureaucratic decision-making process*

The newly evolving analysis of bureaucracy by economists provides more rigorous underpinning for an old conclusion popularly known as 'Parkinson's Law'.[1] Bureaucrats (like anyone else) maximise their own utility, and the principal 'variable' in their 'utility function', or, in plain English, what they mainly want, is power. Power can be roughly measured by a proxy such as the size of the bureaucrat's budget, or the size of his department by the number of employees. Bureaucrats identify themselves with the stated goals of their department, and achieve their satisfactions in life in large part by expanding their activity. They will also therefore strongly resist any attempt to 'dismantle' a government organisation.

(c) *The budgetary process*

A related explanation of continued increase in government expenditure focusses on the budgetary process itself, through which the increases must be achieved. The budgetary process is necessarily fragmented and incremental, primarily because of the human limits on calculability:

'. . . all participants in budgeting are overwhelmed by its complexity. None can relate the myriad factors to one another simultaneously so as to achieve desired allocations. . . . All adopt aids to calculation. All simplify the task of decision by proceeding from an historical base, largely accepting what has gone before, in order to concentrate on proposed new increments.'[2]

At no time is the budget effectively considered as a whole to relate its parts systematically to one another. Thus, the proposals for longer-run planning of government expenditure by planning-programming-budgeting systems and zero-based budgeting[3] have failed to moderate burgeoning government spending. New approaches continue to surface; clearly the central difficulty of controlling government expenditure persists.

[1] William A. Niskanen, *Bureaucracy: Servant or Master?*, Hobart Paperback 5, IEA, 1973; and Gordon Tullock, *The Vote Motive*, Hobart Paperback 9, IEA, 1976, particularly Chapter IV.

[2] Aaron Wildavsky, *Budgeting*, Little Brown, Boston, 1975, p. 9.

[3] Conventional budgeting usually takes the previous year's expenditure on any activity as the base, and considers increments to it. Zero-based budgeting scrutinises the whole activity afresh, in principle ignoring past commitments and obligations.

(d) Cabinet decision-making

Western-style Cabinets comprise an overwhelming majority of Ministers representing 'spending' departments; there is usually only one (the Chancellor) with direct responsibility for raising revenue through taxation. Moreover, even Ministers whose departments are not large spenders will tend to support the majority. A senior British Treasury official spilled the beans neatly:

> 'Who will you get as "non-spending" ministers. The Foreign Minister? He knows he needs the support of his Cabinet colleagues for things he wants to do, even if he's not spending a lot of money.'[1]

Spending Ministers win political bouquets through spending more. Thus, their large majority in Cabinet will generate a bias towards over-expansion of the government sector. Is it inevitable?

(e) So why is Britain (almost) alone in a fiscal crisis?

This Cabinet decision-making process applies in general to most Western Governments.[2] Why then is it Britain, alone of all developed countries (with the possible exception of Italy), that is facing a fiscal crisis of the dimensions indicated by Table VIII?

(An heroic attempt was made by the British Treasury in *Economic Trends* (May 1975) to demonstrate that Britain's government deficit was not all that large in relation to other selected European countries. Their estimates were deficient in two respects. First, they ignored the financing of the investment expenditures of the nationalised industries and other public corporations, variations in which are an important instrument of fiscal policy in Britain. Moreover, the pricing policies of the public corporations which affect their trading surpluses and therefore their borrowing requirements are often determined in the light of general government policy objectives rather than by strict commercial criteria *as in most other countries*. Second, the estimates excluded government lending to the rest of the economy and the overseas sector. This exclusion is not warranted in Britain since such lending is used, *inter alia*, to provide financial support to faltering enterprises and has therefore important policy implications.)

---

[1] Quoted in Hugh Heclo and Aaron Wildavsky, *The Private Government of Public Money*, Macmillan, London, 1974, pp. 186-7.

[2] One fundamental difference is discussed below, (*f*).

TABLE VIII

PUBLIC SECTOR DEFICIT: BRITAIN, 1972-73 to 1976-77

Financial Year	Public Sector Deficit (−)		Full Employment Public Sector Deficit (−)	
	Amount (£ million)	Per cent of GDP	Amount (£ million)	Per cent of Full Employment GDP[a]
1972-3	−2,516	−4·4	−1,170	−2·0
1973-4	−4,458	−7·0	−2,670	−4·1
1974-5	−7,926	−10·2	−4,600	−5·7
1975-6	−10,773	−11·3	−4,330	−4·2
1976-7	−11,962	−10·9	−7,250	−6·1

(a) Estimate of the GDP that would have been realised had the economy been running continuously at full employment.

Sources: Central Statistical Office, Financial Statistics and Economic Trends. Data for the full employment deficit and GDP are taken from National Institute Economic Review, August 1976. GDP at current prices has been assumed to increase by 15 per cent in 1976-77.

The first two columns show the public sector deficit in absolute terms and as a percentage of GDP. The data indicate an almost continual deterioration since 1972-73, with the deficit expected to reach almost £12 billion in 1976-77, approximately 11 per cent of GDP.

To obtain a picture of the underlying performance of fiscal policy, the data is adjusted for fluctuations in economic activity. When the economy is operating below capacity, a deficit will tend to emerge as tax receipts fall and some items of government expenditure (such as unemployment benefits) increase. The 'full employment deficit' attempts to remove these influences; it is the deficit that would have occurred had revenues and expenditures been based on full employment incomes. These data (last two columns of Table VIII) indicate a similar deteriorating performance, from 2·0 per cent of GDP in 1972-73 to 6·1 per cent in 1976-77. It is this trend that indicates a fiscal crisis in Britain, and explains why the Government has finally been forced to acknowledge that the country can indulge no real increase in government expenditure before 1979-80.[1]

[1] Public Expenditure to 1979-80, HMSO, February 1976, p. 2.

How has this massive imbalance been allowed to occur? One crucial element must be the uniqueness of the British budgetary system.

(f) Not so much a budget, more an expenditure catalogue
A dictionary definition of 'budget' is:

'A plan or schedule adjusting expenses during a certain period to the estimated or fixed income for that period.'[1]

In neither the letter nor the spirit of this definition does the British Government have a budget. What the Government has is not a scheme to spend what it can raise in taxes but an expenditure catalogue drawn up and executed with *a disregard of 'income for that period' that is unparalleled among developed economies*:

'In Britain the main expenditure decisions are taken in advance of the Budget and the Budget itself usually deals exclusively with taxation. In other countries the Budget covers both expenditure and taxation.

Are there weaknesses in the British procedure? Does it mean that expenditure decisions are taken in advance of the economic forecasts underlying the Budget and that these decisions are not seen alongside their tax implications?'[2]

Sir Alec Cairncross (former head of the Government Economic Service) answered his own questions in testimony to the Expenditure Committee:

'I think there is something a little awkward about an arrangement under which . . . changes in expenditure are sometimes considered in relation to one another . . . but independently of the taxation to which they may give rise.'[3]

The formulation of expenditure estimates for the financial year begins more than 12 months in advance. In late February the Treasury collects estimates of expenditure for the current year, the coming budget year, and three subsequent years. These estimates are discussed with Treasury officials and passed to an inter-departmental Public Expenditure Survey Committee (PESC) which prepares a final report for Cabinet scrutiny between July and November. The Cabinet decisions

[1] *Webster's New World Dictionary*, World Publishing Company, New York, 1972, p. 184.

[2] Sir Alec Cairncross, in *First Report of the Expenditure Committee*, HMSO, December 1975, p. 20.

[3] *Ibid.*, p. 22.

are published in the Public Expenditure White Paper (usually in December or January), and comprise the expenditure side of the central Government's budget in March or April.

But, the reader moved by common sense will ask, surely the Cabinet considers the expenditure estimates in the light of the taxation consequences? With one exception (discussed below) it seems this has *not* been done, at least from 1964 to 1970. Lord Diamond, Chief Secretary to the Treasury (whose main Cabinet responsibility was for public expenditure), goes to great lengths to separate the two issues:

'It is necessary to understand that although public expenditure is of great social, economic and political importance, and although it is mainly financed out of taxation, the decisions about taxation are taken in a different context, the economic one. . . . It is necessary to point out this simple truth in view of a tendency to *confuse the relative functions of the Budget and Public Expenditure Survey Committee (PESC) exercises.*'[1]

Indeed, Lord Diamond carries his argument to the logical conclusion, arguing that the *de facto* separation of expenditure and revenue decisions be formalised by hiving-off the Treasury's government expenditure functions into a new Public Expenditure Department.

(g) Cabinet and the spending Ministers

It could be argued that a preponderance of spending Ministers in Cabinet is not a sufficient condition for expenditure to be bloated. Why do spending Ministers not attack one another's programmes rather than form a united front against the Chancellor? In countries where the target variable is the budget deficit, this is likely to occur; and where there is a clear limit for total government expenditure. *Neither condition holds in Britain.* The total expenditure limit passed on from PESC to the Cabinet is anything but firm, and always emerges from the Cabinet room substantially higher than it went in.[2] The British Cabinet process does not encourage 'trade-offs' among expenditure proposals of the Ministers:

'Finally and overarching all other barriers to weighing expenditures against each other are the behavioural norms against mutual

[1] *Public Expenditure in Practice*, Allen & Unwin, 1975, p. 66 (my italics). The planning of government expenditure in real terms also makes it difficult to relate the expenditure data to required cash revenues.

[2] Heclo and Wildavsky, *op. cit.*, pp. 169-97, and Lord Diamond, *op. cit.*, pp. 51-99.

attack. Greasings by civil service society will already have muted most interdepartmental squeaks before Cabinet meetings. Department briefings will do their best to prepare the minister for protecting his own case but offer little scope for analysing others' claims.

Reciprocity in ministerial discussions (you leave my programs alone and I'll leave yours alone) is the counterpart of reciprocal neutrality among civil servants in relation to each other's spending. Spending ministers' reluctance to criticise each other's proposals is a standing guarantee that the sequence of decisions usually will not be disturbed by explicit trade-offs or cross-references.'[1]

(h) Implications of separating expenditure and tax decisions

What are the consequences of taking expenditure decisions where the amount and the distribution of taxes are settled wholly apart? Cabinet will tend to vote for an expansion of expenditures to the point where their evaluation of the additional ('marginal') benefits becomes zero. This behaviour is not unrealistic and is not confined to Cabinet. Much discussion in the popular press and among academics concerned with welfare concerns 'needs' for new or expanded public services. Almost universally these 'needs' are measured or estimated independently of costs. The outcome of this division of decisions is clear:

'The direction of bias seems evident. The splitting of the fiscal decision into two parts tends to cause a "deficit" between approved spending rates and approved tax rates. Insofar as the expenditure decision fails to take into account the cost side, public services provided will tend to be extended beyond that level which fully informed consideration of alternatives would produce.

Conversely, insofar as the tax decision fails to incorporate the benefit side, total tax revenues will fall short of the amount needed to finance that level of public services that an informed consideration of alternatives would provide.

In other words, the gap between approved spending and approved taxes will tend to "straddle" the unique tax-spending solution that an "efficient" fiscal decision might produce.'[2]

The resultant deficit might be expected to bring to the surface the interdependence of expenditure and tax decisions, and

---

[1] Heclo and Wildavsky, op. cit., p. 190.

[2] James M. Buchanan, Public Finance in Democratic Process, Chapel Hill, North Carolina, 1967, p. 92.

resolve the contradiction. The data in Table VIII indicate that this has not happened in Britain. Why not?—for two related yet distinct reasons: Keynesianism and inflation.

(i) Keynes's legacy and fiscal illusion

Keynes demonstrated that the budget need not be balanced year in year out, nor indeed in any year. During periods of depressed activity, a deficit would be induced (frequently financed by money creation) and this (or indeed a larger) deficit was appropriate for short-term management of aggregate demand. Conversely, during boom periods, a budget surplus would be appropriate. *Keynesian policy weakened the link between expenditure and taxation in the minds of politicians and the public.* It encouraged the idea that governments should and can create money to pay for public services. Both notions stimulated the delusion that government expenditures are not in reality constrained by tax revenues.

The evidence of recent years in Britain that money can be created by government has encouraged the view of politicians as miracle-doers. If government can create money, it can do anything. With this psychology, it is a small and fatal step to the belief that, if the government is not willing to do something, it is not because it cannot 'afford' to, but rather because it does not believe that the something is worth doing, but can be persuaded it is if the pressure is strong enough. Thus arises the fiscal illusion which has led the British people to believe that government dispenses gifts through a supra-human Santa Claus from whose bottomless sack more and more can be produced without charge to anyone.

(j) Fiscal illusion through inflation

Where inflation increases *money* incomes, politicians may suffer from the illusion that a higher proportion of the revenue represents increases in *real* incomes. They may then tend to spend the automatic increases in money revenues on expanding the relative size of the government sector. Given the inflationary experience of Britain in recent times, it is difficult to under-estimate the potential importance of this illusion. Total personal tax revenues in Britain in 1975-76 were over £15,000 million, *more than double those only two years earlier.*[1] 'Public' sector expenditure as a percentage of GDP at factor cost increased from

---

[1] £15,068 million for 1975-76; £7,058 million for 1973-74. (*Financial Statement and Budget Report*, 1974-75 and 1976-77, p. 19 in both.)

52·9 to 59·5 per cent, despite *zero* growth in *real* GDP. Inflation averaged 18·6 per cent over the three years.

If inflation continues at 1975-76 rates the 'natural' growth of personal tax revenues would provide another doubling within two years. With such rates of increase, politicians can easily be deluded into thinking the revenue constraint is not all that 'tight'.

(k) Indexation: a bridge between expenditure and taxes
The one circumstance in which Lord Diamond acknowledged tax considerations would enter into the Cabinet's public expenditure deliberations was when the public expenditure proposals

> '. . . add up to *new tax legislation* and . . . there is a figure beyond which the consequential *additional tax proposals* are politically unacceptable.'[1]

There was no mention of increasing real tax rates or an increased tax burden, but only of a situation where *new* proposals and *explicit* legislation are required. An unindexed tax schedule thus camouflages the tax consequences of increased government expenditures. Successive British Chancellors have been able to get away with *seemingly* modest explicit increases in marginal tax *rates*, and been able to combine them with heavily emphasised but bogus tax 'cuts'—increases in dependent allowances that do not even restore their original real values.

Indexation would require all *real* increases in tax rates to be legislated explicitly, rather than be produced through the back door of inflation. To obtain the same revenues with indexation since, say, 1973-74, Chancellors would have had either explicitly to *decrease* the personal allowance, the married person's allowance, child allowances, and the width of taxable income brackets from their inflation-adjusted values, or maintain those values and further increase marginal tax rates. Also, given the zero growth in real income since 1973-74, the British Cabinet would have become increasingly aware that *any* increase in the relative size of the government sector would have required what Lord Diamond called 'additional tax proposals': in plain English, tax increases openly announced and debated in Parliament.

Had the required tax increases been considered politically unacceptable, the Cabinet would have been faced with two

[1] *Op. cit.,* p. 65 (my italics).

options: to run a still larger deficit financed by money creation (or borrowing),[1] or to reduce proposed government spending. The first option would be considerably less attractive under an indexed system, since the resulting increased inflation would not yield the windfall of tax receipts of a non-indexed system.[2]

Indexation would thus do much to eradicate the fiscal illusions of politicians and the public. Increased government expenditures would be subject to more Cabinet, Parliamentary, and public scrutiny—which is highly desirable since they are now based on a substantially increased government sector relative to that less than a decade ago.[3] It is also appropriate to a society that professes to be democratic and open.

Indexation need not necessarily imply a smaller public sector. The Cabinet, Parliament, and even the public might support increasing government expenditures even when confronted openly with the tax increases. But the public would have the ultimate power to decide. Recent resistance to increasing tax rates (take-home pay bargaining, increased tax avoidance and evasion[4]) suggests a lack of public support for current volumes of government spending. The most likely outcome of indexation in Britain is therefore a smaller government sector.

Indexation is also likely to encourage a more efficient government sector, with new expenditure stimulating a review of past expenditures.

4. Revenue implications: can Britain 'afford' indexation?
Given the magnitude of the gap between revenue and expenditure, can Britain afford indexation now? The current plan of

---

[1] From the non-bank public or overseas, but these sources were already under substantial strain. Borrowing from the non-bank public by the government increased by £2,500 million in 1973-74 and by £4,300 million in 1974-75. Outstanding official overseas debt (short- and medium-term) increased from £3,000 million at the end of 1973 to more than £7,000 million at the end of 1974, and to just under £9,000 million at the end of 1975. (Bank of England *Quarterly Bulletin* and Central Statistical Office, *Financial Statistics*.)

[2] The government yield from inflation would be confined to the tax on cash balances, and (before the introduction of inflation-adjusted stock appreciation provisions) increased company tax receipts.

[3] Government expenditure as a proportion of GDP at factor cost increased from 50·1 per cent in 1969-70 to 59·5 per cent in 1975-76. (Central Statistical Office, *Financial Statistics* and *Economic Trends*.)

[4] It is difficult to obtain evidence on the extent of increased avoidance and evasion. The Inland Revenue thinks that both have increased considerably in recent years: examination of Inland Revenue officials in *First Report From the Expenditure Committee, 1975-76*, HMSO, 1975, pp. 182-3.

the Government is to reduce the ratio of public expenditure to GDP from 59·5 per cent in 1975-76 to 53 per cent in 1979-80[1] by holding the 1976-77 expenditure constant in real terms. The tax ratio will still have to be increased to reduce the underlying deficit to manageable proportions. Could it be achieved under indexation?

The answer depends on the elasticity of British taxes in response to changes in *real* income. For the moment, inflation will be ignored. Under an indexed tax system, *real* income increases will continue to attract higher average tax rates. Income tax receipts were projected to constitute one-third of total government receipts in 1976-77.[2] If the real income elasticity is 1·75 and of all other taxes unity (a 1 per cent increase in real income will generate a 1 per cent increase in other taxes), the elasticity of the tax system as a whole is 1.25.[3]

Applying this elasticity to the growth rate of 3·4 per cent assumed in the 1976 Public Expenditure White Paper implies that the ratio of government receipts to GDP at factor cost will increase from 48·3 per cent in 1975-76 to 50 per cent in 1979-80. This would leave a deficit of 3 per cent of GDP in 1979-80, which it should be possible to finance from non-inflationary sources.[4]

Inflation would affect these calculations very little. Under indexation, inflation will leave the real value of income tax receipts unaltered—government will neither gain nor lose real-income tax receipts. Given current stock appreciation and depreciation provisions, the same holds true of corporate tax receipts. What will be required is discretionary action to maintain the real value of specific excise duties by increasing them with inflation.

In brief, indexation can be 'afforded' on *present* expenditure plans. Its main contribution would be to help ensure that government holds to these plans.

[1] *Public Expenditure to 1979-80*, HMSO, 1976, p. 8.

[2] *Financial Statement and Budget Report, 1976-77*, HMSO, 1976, pp. 14-19.

[3] The elasticity of the income tax is equal to the ratio of the marginal tax rate to the average tax rate. In 1976-77 the average wage-earner will have a marginal rate of 35 per cent and an average rate of approximately 17·5 per cent, implying an elasticity of two. This elasticity will decline over the period as the average tax rate on average earnings increases.

[4] An average deficit of this magnitude was sustained from 1964 to 1968. (Robert Neild and Terry Ward, 'The Budget Deficit in Perspective', *The Times*, 12 July, 1976.)

5. Implications for macro-economic stability

The report of the Canadian Royal Commission on Taxation, which did not feel able to recommend automatic indexation, argued that to tax only increases in real purchasing power would irreparably damage the built-in stability of the system. The results of extensive testing with econometric models for the US, Canadian and Australian economies do not support this argument,[1] but appear to be consistent with casual empiricism based on observations of macro-economic stability in developed economies that have adopted indexation and whose economic performance suggests that economic stability (of prices, employment) has more to do with the appropriateness of discretionary macro-economic policies (such as the control of monetary aggregates) than with whether the personal tax system is indexed or not.

It may be objected that econometric models are ill-equipped to depict accurately the likely influence of indexation on the rate of inflation, in particular that existing wage equations in econometric models do not reflect recent developments in wage bargaining on take-home pay. They may also be unable to capture various psychological changes that could accompany the introduction of indexation.

(a) Wage retaliation against increased taxation

Keynesian theory said that an increase in tax rates reduces private sector take-home pay and consumption expenditure and, *via* the multiplier process, reduces national income. Profit-maximising behaviour by producers then leads to lower output, employment and prices. The tax increase may therefore be considered deflationary, since it reduces the equilibrium level of prices. The crucial assumption is that the money wage-rate remains constant in the short run.[2]

Recent experience in several developed economies (Austria, Canada, Finland, Germany, Ireland, Sweden, Britain and the United States) has suggested that Keynesian theory may be rather too simplistic, because employees are essentially concerned with take-home rather than gross pay and try to offset

---

[1] J. Bossons and T. A. Wilson, 'Adjusting Tax Rates for Inflation', *Canadian Tax Journal*, March-April 1973; *Report of Committee of Inquiry Into Inflation and Taxation, op. cit.*, and H. Aaron *et al*, *Inflation and Taxation*, The Brookings Institution, Washington DC, 1977.

[2] The analysis also assumes that the increased taxes do not lead to increased government expenditure.

higher taxation by gross wage increases.[1] This hypothesis has been confirmed for Britain over 1948-74 in five models of inflation subjected to extensive econometric testing.[2]

To examine the role (if any) indexation can play in mitigating wage retaliation against higher taxation, we must consider the underlying *rationale* for retaliation (particularly under inflationary conditions), the macro-economic implications, and the required policy.

(b) Wage retaliation during inflation

An increased average tax rate may result from higher real income or higher money income that merely compensates for inflation (Section II). Wage retaliation can be expected to be stronger during inflation since an increase in *real* gross (pre-tax) wages can be translated into an absolute *decrease* in real take-home pay. When prices are stable, *any* increase in pre-tax wages also increases real take-home pay (assuming marginal tax rates are below 100 per cent!).

(c) Rationales for wage retaliation

To assess the impact of indexation on wage inflation, we must examine the *rationale* of wage retaliation. Jackson, Turner, and Wilkinson have argued that the 'wage explosion' of 1970 and 1971 was sparked off by *inflation-induced* tax increases on lower incomes.[3] They suggest this development was directly contrary to the stated TUC policy of achieving preferential treatment for the lower paid (who were being dragged into the tax net by inflation), and was important in provoking widespread industrial unrest and subsequent inflationary wage settlements.

Another possible *rationale* is that inflation increases taxes beyond the amounts explicitly agreed through the political process, and changes the distribution of the tax burden. It may be argued that there is less resentment against *unlegislated* than against legislated increases. A minor variant of this argument,

[1] OECD, *The Adjustment of Personal Income Tax Systems for Inflation*, OECD, Paris, 1976, pp. 25-6; Dernburg, *op. cit.*; Robert J. Gordon, 'Inflation in Recession and Recovery', *Brookings Papers on Economic Activity*, No. 1, 1971; and Jackson, Turner and Wilkinson, *op. cit.*

[2] Henry, Sawyer and Smith, *op. cit.*, p. 60. Further empirical support for 1952-71 may be found in Johnson and Timbrell, *op. cit.*

[3] *Op. cit.*, pp. 93-4.

the 'surprise' hypothesis, has been proffered by Bacon and Eltis. They argue that in Britain between 1961 and 1974 there was a

'. . . lack of knowledge by the people at election time of the extra costs of higher social spending that they themselves would have to pay . . . the full taxation costs . . . were never made clear enough. The British people therefore voted for higher social spending, and then set off rapid wage inflation when they realised to their surprise that they were expected to pay for it.'[1]

(d) The social wage debate

When expenditure increases do not accompany tax increases, the *rationale* for wage retaliation seems straightforward:

'. . . bigger *gross* wage increases were required to maintain the accustomed rise of real *net* earnings—or even, for many groups, to prevent real living standards from falling.'[2]

But when the tax increase is associated with increased government expenditure (as in Britain, certainly since 1969-70), decreases in real take-home pay cannot be equated with decreases in real living standards—it becomes necessary to consider the 'social wage' (defined by Mr Healey in his 1975-76 Budget speech as the money value of government expenditure per head of the working population). What do trade union attempts to avoid increased taxation (by bargaining on take-home pay) imply about their attitude towards the social wage?

The short answer indicated by the econometric evidence (sub-section (a)) can only be that *unions find the social wage completely irrelevant to their wage negotiations*. If unions were simply unaware of the increased government expenditure made possible by higher taxation, the solution would be straightforward—public education. The problem would seem to be more serious.

First, unions may not regard expansion of government expenditure as of substantial benefit to themselves, in part because the taxpayer and the beneficiary of public services may not be the same person, in part because increases in government expenditure (inputs) have not been matched by

---

[1] Robert Bacon and Walter Eltis, *Britain's Economic Problem: Too Few Producers*, Macmillan, London, 1976, p. 101.

[2] Jackson, Turner and Wilkinson, *op. cit.*, p. 102.

improvements in real per capita government services (outputs). Government expenditure statistics reflect payments for inputs, not production of outputs. When an attempt is made to quantify government outputs in services like education and health, increasing money inputs are frequently associated with stagnant or even declining real outputs.[1]

Second, even if unions do perceive increased benefits flowing from additional government expenditures, there is still the so-called 'free rider'* difficulty. An individual union may believe that avoidance of increased taxation by its members will not jeopardise the general increase in government expenditure. Hence, it is consistent for the TUC to espouse the merits of the 'social wage', while individual unions negotiate for private take-home pay with their employers.

The wishes of incomes policy negotiators to the contrary, Britain has a highly decentralised system of wage bargaining:

> 'The rise of shop stewards and the willingness of many managers to bargain with them has shifted the focus of bargaining. The authority of the unions over their stewards and members is diminished by the diversity of their structures and competition between them, and most . . . have not a quarter of the full-time officers necessary to maintain effective contact with the plants.'[2]

(e) Macro-economic implications of wage retaliation

Keynesian theory indicates that an increase in taxes will reduce demand, prices, output, and employment.[3] Wage retaliation against higher taxation raises the equilibrium price level and accentuates the fall in output and employment. If governments' commitment to full employment leads to an accommodating monetary policy that underwrites the inflationary increase in gross wages, the accentuated fall in output and employment will be reduced, but at the cost of a further rise in the price level. The more the wage retaliation, the larger the required increase in the money supply to offset the employment effect.

[1] Bacon and Eltis, op. cit., pp. 14-15.

[2] Hugh Clegg, How to run an Incomes Policy and Why we Made Such a Mess of the Last One, Heinemann, London, 1971, p. 79.

[3] Assuming again that the increase in taxes does not generate increased government expenditure.

* Glossary.

(f) Policy against stagflation: tight-money, low-taxation
With or without an accompanying increase in the money
supply, wage retaliation tends to produce 'stagflation'—
declining real output and rising prices. If the government
expands the money supply, the decrease in output tends to be
lower, and the increase in the price level higher, than if money
supply is kept constant. Recent British experience indicates
that wage increases have almost always been underwritten
by an expansion of the money supply.[1] With what result?

The stagflation generated by wage retaliation can be considered the result of excessive taxes and money supply. The
policy adjustments indicated are a reduction in the money
supply and in personal taxes. These adjustments, derived
theoretically by Dernburg,[2] have also been indicated by
empirical work in the United States.[3] What contribution could
indexation make to achieve this policy?

(g) Tax indexation and wage retaliation
The main aim of British trade unions in wage negotiations
for much of the post-war period has been to secure a 2 to $2\frac{1}{2}$ per
cent per annum increase in real take-home pay.[4] Increasing
taxation has raised the required *gross* wage increase necessary
to secure this target. Unions have generally been successful in
obtaining the required gross wage settlement, and successive
governments have underwritten them through an accommodating monetary policy. The results, indicated by theory and
confirmed by experience, are a higher price level and possibly
lower real output than would have emerged had there been
no wage retaliation. The econometric evidence suggests that

'. . . income tax concessions raising real net take-home pay would
slow down money wage increases.'[5]

Indexation could contribute towards the appropriate policy
mix by reducing the required increase in *gross* wages to achieve
the target increase in real take-home pay. Indexation means
that maintaining real gross pay during inflation will also
maintain real take-home pay, assuming, of course, that

---

[1] Ralph Harris, in *British Economic Policy 1970-74*, Hobart Paperback 7, IEA,
1975.

[2] *Op. cit.*

[3] R. J. Gordon, *op. cit.*, p. 132.

[4] Derived from Henry, Sawyer, and Smith, *op. cit.*, p. 69.

[5] *Ibid.*, p. 70.

[69]

indexation is not accompanied by discretionary tax-rate increases.[1]

(h) Wage retaliation and resource transfer to the government
What happens when the increased taxes are used to finance additional government spending? Conventionally, balanced budget expansion increases the equilibrium level of output, employment and prices, the additional government resources being obtained in part by increased output, in part by reduced real private consumption and investment. When balanced budget expansion is accompanied by wage retaliation:

> 'the result . . . is something of a nightmare. The price level is . . . pulled [upward] by the aggregate demand effect of the policies and pushed by the wage adjustment . . . Furthermore, wage adjustment tends to reduce output and the reduction in real consumption and real investment will therefore be magnified by [it], even though it is the intention of wage adjustment to prevent a fall in real consumption.'[2]

The appropriate policy is to finance increased expenditures by borrowing from the non-bank private sector, and run a restrictive monetary policy.[3] The difficulty with this policy mix is that more of the resources are likely to be transferred from investment.

Tax indexation must operate by reducing wage retaliation, or by inducing a reconsideration of the new expenditure programmes (or of old programmes that could make way for the new). Indexation, accompanied by a discretionary increase in taxation, may reduce wage retaliation. It may do so if unions retaliate against the adverse *distribution* of the tax increase caused by inflation, or if the tax increase comes as a surprise, so that it is not presented to the electorate as required for increased expenditures, and is not legislated explicitly. If neither mitigates wage retaliation, indexation must operate by inducing moderation in the rate of growth of government outlays (discussed above).

[1] It is interesting to note the Labour Government's changing attitude towards the role of personal taxation as an anti-wage inflation instrument. In his 1975-76 Budget Mr Healey increased income tax as an 'anti-wage inflation surcharge' (*Hansard*, 15 April 1975, column 317). Twelve months later, with average earnings having increased by 18 per cent, he was proposing 'cuts' in personal taxation in an effort to restrain wage inflation.

[2] Dernburg, *op. cit.*, pp. 784-5.

[3] *Ibid.*, p. 785.

(i) Should indexation be part of an incomes policy?
The 1976-77 Budget, in which the Chancellor traded-off tax concessions in return for TUC promises on wage restraint, raised the question whether indexation should be made conditional upon agreement to an incomes policy by the unions. It should not.

First, indexation may yield some moderation of gross wage increases, but the main arguments for indexation are tax equity, making tax increases explicit, reducing government's net benefit from inflation, and inducing restraint in government expenditure. 'Off-again, on-again' indexation puts these benefits at risk. It also puts the possible benefit of wage moderation at risk. There is often a lengthy lag between the formulation of a wage claim and its settlement. Hence, it requires forecasting of the tax rates, deductions and allowances in force when the new pay rates come into effect. Indexation does not rule out discretionary adjustments to tax rates and deductions. Nevertheless, *automatic* indexation does make the most reasonable expectation to be one of constant rather than increasing real rates of tax.

(j) Price stability as a public good
Secondly, in entering into an incomes policy, successive governments have given up much and, on the available evidence, gained little or nothing in return. Extensive econometric testing for Britain has concluded:

> '. . . when wage controls are operating, the average wage inflation over the control period is not significantly different from what would be predicted in the absence of controls.'[1]

This is scarcely surprising given the decentralised wage bargaining system in Britain. Even if price stability was universally desired, incomes policy is unlikely to achieve any sustained moderation of wage claims in highly decentralised bargaining such as in Britain. The problem is an example of making a decision about a 'public good'[2] (namely price stability). If the

---

[1] David Laidler and Michael Parkin, 'Inflation: A Survey', *Economic Journal*, December 1975, p. 763. Henry, Sawyer, and Smith, *op. cit.*, found only one incomes policy from 1949 to 1973 to be effective.

[2] A 'public good' is one of which the consumption by one individual does not reduce the quantity available for consumption by others, and where non-payers cannot be excluded from the benefits.

number of bargaining units is large, no one of them would make a significant contribution to obtaining the public good by limiting its own wage increases. Unless acting in concert with a large number of others, it would be acting not only altruistically but also foolishly in limiting them.[1]

(k) The costs of incomes policies

It would not matter much if incomes policies were simply ineffective. But they entail substantial costs, making them positively harmful. These costs include:

(i) Price controls, which are far more 'effectively' pursued than wage controls. Incomes policies can take a good deal of the 'credit' for the reduction in the pre-tax rate of return on industrial investment to 4·0 per cent in 1974; and to *minus* 0·3 per cent for the post-tax return.[2]

(ii) Incomes policies are usually regarded as a substitute for responsible monetary and fiscal policy (e.g. Mr Barber's boom of 1972-73).

(iii) Formal TUC support is usually bought at the cost of accepting such self-defeating policies (from the point of view of inflation control) as food subsidies and price freezes for nationalised industries. Making tax indexation part of an incomes policy would inhibit the ability to accompany it with discretionary tax increases. Indexation is a social contract between *all* taxpayers, not only unionists; it requires an agreement by the government to legislate tax increases explicitly rather than introduce them through the back door of inflation.

(iv) Tax increases based on non-economic grounds, being explicitly introduced as a means of securing the acquiescence of certain groups to other changes. Mr Healey's 'soaking the rich' by economically damaging (certainly to the Inland Revenue) marginal tax rates—up to 98 per cent—is an obvious recent example.

(l) The wrong lessons from 1976-77

There is a good chance that the wrong lessons will be learnt from 1976-77, with Mr Healey concluding that conditional indexation in the context of incomes policy with the TUC is

---

[1] This argument is elaborated in D. H. Whitehead, *Stagflation and Wages Policy in Australia,* Longman, Victoria, 1973, pp. 91-2.

[2] Bank of England, *Quarterly Bulletin,* March 1976.

the way forward. Moderate wage increases in 1976-77 will have little if anything to do with TUC support. To the extent that wage increases are moderate, that will be due in part to the tax cuts, in part to the highest unemployment rate since the 1930s (5·3 per cent in June 1976, excluding school leavers), and in part to the possibility of a relatively moderate increase in the money supply.

(m) Indexation and attitudes towards inflation

It has been suggested that indexation may produce a general public impression that the government expects inflation to continue and, therefore, may induce scepticism about the effectiveness of anti-inflationary measures.[1] Consequently, it is argued, inflationary expectations will increase, and may become self-fulfilling.

A related argument concentrates on the psychological reaction of governments to the introduction of indexation: that it may result in a lower urgency being given to controlling inflation because of the belief that the personal taxpayer is more or less immune from the detrimental effects of inflation. Government may believe that a fall in the value of money has been made easily tolerable.

Both arguments would seem more relevant to economy-wide indexing (wages, interest rates, all taxes and transfer payments).[2] In developed economies indexation of one element does not appear to have led to a philosophical commitment towards economy-wide indexation.

Personal tax indexation would remove one source of discontent with inflation, but discontent with inflation has at least as much to do with 'social' as with economic factors; inflation is likely to remain socially and politically unpopular. Indexation is likely to generate a less complacent attitude by government towards inflation by reducing the net benefits flowing to it.

Indexation will not remove all sources of government revenue from inflation (for example, the reduction in the real value of government debt, and the inflation tax on cash balances), but would eliminate the major one.

---

[1] OECD, *The Adjustment of Personal Income Tax Systems for Inflation, op. cit.*, p. 17.

[2] These arguments are considered in detail by Jackman and Klappholz, *op. cit.*

VI. CONCLUSIONS FOR POLICY

The experience of virtually every OECD country over the past five years or so confirms that during relatively rapid inflation the issue is not *whether* to adjust the personal tax schedule but *how*. The question is whether adjustment should occur automatically each year, or be left to government to make *ad hoc* adjustments from time to time.

1. *Ad hoc versus automatic adjustment*

In an ultimate but very real sense, there can never be 'fully automatic' indexation, as the Netherlands showed in 1974 when it suspended the adjustment mechanism. The automatic nature of legislative provisions does not change the ultimate power of government to suspend the laws of the day if it sees fit.[1] No legislation can remove this power, nor does it aim to do so. Yet such an option does not render 'automatic' indexation irrelevant or unimportant. The existence of such provisions ensures that failure to adjust taxes for inflation in any given year is an explicit government decision requiring public justification. This is not so in a system of *ad hoc* adjustment.

In essence, the choice between automatic and *ad hoc* adjustment rests on this difference. Automatic adjustment involves the undertaking that inflation will not be allowed to increase the real tax burden automatically beyond the weight explicitly agreed to by the political process. It further involves the undertaking that increases in taxes will be subjected to parliamentary and public scrutiny. In this sense automatic indexation ensures more accountability by government to the taxpayer.

The delay between inflation and adjustment of income tax tends to be longer and more erratic when *ad hoc* adjustment methods are used. They are likely to have less of a moderating influence on trade union attitudes to wage negotiations because they are uncertain and delayed. Automatic adjustment tends to minimise the need for the large infrequent adjustments often associated with *ad hoc* adjustment. Automatic adjustment may be viewed as providing a more gradual, smoother process of adjustment.

2. *Short-term politics and long-term economics*

Given the case for adjustment, the governmental decision-

---

[1] Equally, non-adjustment may be viewed as indexation plus additional discretionary adjustments that precisely offset the adjustment for inflation.

making process may be facilitated when there is a commitment to adjust regularly in the framework of specific legislation. Automatic adjustment should provide government with a clearer picture of its share of resources over the longer term if existing tax policies continue. During periods of persistent and relatively rapid inflation, maintenance of the current *real* rate scale is a workable assumption, though less tenable for maintenance of the current *money* rate schedule. Use of the latter assumption may imply, in the short term, a governmental claim over resources that may be difficult to sustain over the longer term given the necessity to effect significant future *ad hoc* adjustments. Hence the possibility of expenditure decisions being taken in the short run (particularly during rapid inflation, such as food subsidies and subsidies to nationalised industries) that may create problems for the large *ad hoc* adjustments required to be made in the future to offset the effects of inflation.

3. *Indexation during moderate inflation*

Introducing formal indexation during a period of rapid inflation might be objected to on the grounds that, once implemented, it would be extremely difficult to remove when conditions changed, so that it may be regarded as at least largely unnecessary, if not inappropriate. That argument is valid to the extent that indexation, once adopted, is extremely unlikely to be abandoned. But it is not clear why, during periods of relatively *low* inflation, it should be a source of concern. Certainly the worst fears of opponents of indexation about 'revenue losses' and stabilisation problems (Section V) should be ameliorated. Moreover, the scheme remains of value to taxpayers since, during periods of relatively low inflation, an unchanged tax schedule is a viable alternative for government. Indeed, some extremely large redistributions of the tax burden in the post-war period arose before the 1970s when the tax schedules of some countries remained largely unchanged in money terms for more than a decade.[1]

[1] The experience of Britain, Australia, Canada, and the US over the period from the early 1950s to the late 1960s confirms this conclusion. (F. W. Paish,'Inflation, Personal Incomes and Taxation', *Lloyds Bank Review*, April 1975; *Personal Income Tax—The Rate Scale*, Australian Government Publishing Service, Canberra, 1974, pp. 9-19; Charles L. Goetz and Warren E. Weber, 'Intertemporal Changes in Real Federal Income Tax Rates, 1954-70', *National Tax Journal*, March 1971; and Vukelich, *op. cit.*)

4. *Implications of increased public awareness*

The rate of inflation, the weight of personal taxation, and the sensitivity of the tax schedule to the distorting effects of inflation would seem to be the more relevant factors in the decision whether to adopt indexation. Other less important, but relevant, factors may include the rate of growth of real incomes, and the ease of making additional discretionary tax adjustments. On all these grounds, conditions in Britain seem particularly appropriate to the introduction of indexation. Those who point out that Britain's tax rates are not the highest among OECD countries should recall that her *per capita* income, an important determinant of 'ability-to-pay' taxes, is among the lowest of OECD countries.

However 'painless' it may have been in the past to increase real tax rates by the combination of inflation and largely unchanged taxes, the option is becoming increasingly less attractive to government. As a result of substantial increases in the rate of recent inflation and in the weight of taxation in many developed countries (and, no doubt, many less developed countries), there has been an increase in the awareness by the taxpaying public of the relationships between inflation, personal taxation and real disposable incomes (take-home pay).

If the combination of inflation and largely unchanged taxation is allowed to continue, this increased awareness is likely to generate responses from taxpayers that will reduce the efficacy of personal taxation as an instrument for counter-inflation policy, for transferring resources to the government sector, and for redistributing income within the private sector. The main responses will be a further spreading of take-home pay bargaining, increased avoidance and evasion, and a quickening decline in taxpayer morality. Whether *ad hoc* adjustments at the discretion of government can be relied upon to prevent or contain such responses is difficult to know. What is known is that an increasing number of countries have, in the comparatively recent past, preferred a more systematic and certain form of adjustment to neutralise the effects of inflation. As long as inflation continues at recent rates, such a trend may be expected to continue.

INFLATION AND THE 1974-75 BUDGET

The proposition advanced by the Chancellor of the Exchequer, Mr Denis Healey, in his 1975 Budget Statement that in 1974-75 inflation raised government expenditure much more than tax receipts appears to conflict with my contention (page 23) that it would reduce the budget deficit or increase the surplus. Mr Healey said:

'. . . when inflation is running at the rates hitherto regarded as normal, it has little significant effect on the balance between public expenditure and receipts. But in the conditions of last year the inflation caused by excessively large wage and salary increases raised public expenditure in money terms much more than public sector receipts, and the public sector deficit rose sharply . . . it must cause one to reflect seriously on the wisdom of planning public expenditure solely on the basis of constant prices.'[1]

The outturn of government expenditure for 1974-75 was 3 per cent higher than the estimated total in November 1974. Much of the increase could be regarded as directly attributable to the unanticipated increase in the rate of inflation. The distinctive feature of this episode lies not with the expenditure response to the unanticipated inflation, but with the revenue response. The outturn of government revenues for 1974-75 was virtually identical with the November 1974 estimate. It is true that a relatively large proportion of total UK tax revenues are accounted for by specific duties on oil, tobacco, and alcoholic beverages (17·5 per cent for 1975-76). Also company tax payments are based on income of the preceding accounting year and hence their real value in the current year would vary inversely with the rate of inflation. The UK personal tax schedule has a very wide first taxable income bracket within which the incomes of the vast majority of personal taxpayers fall. This does not make the personal tax system equivalent to a strictly proportional tax system in the sense that the elasticity of personal taxes to income equals unity.* An average taxpayer in 1974-75 may have been facing a personal tax elasticity of around 1·5.[2] Given the dominance of personal income taxes in total taxation (52 per cent in 1975), it would seem extremely unlikely that the elasticity of the tax system as a whole in response to changes in money income is below unity.

[1] Budget Statement, *Hansard*, 15 April 1975, column 279.

[2] That is, a 10 per cent increase in gross income would have resulted in a 15 per cent increase in personal taxes.

* Glossary .

The major reason for the failure of tax revenue to rise was the substantial increase in unemployment and short-time working in the last five months of the financial year.[1] The problem was not primarily one of a tax system extremely unresponsive to changes in money income, but rather that money incomes in total increased only moderately. Rapid increases in wage-rates were accompanied by a substantial decrease in the volume of employment.[2] If the government sector shared fully in the increased unemployment, some reduction in government expenditures would have offset the reduction in the aggregate personal tax base. However, it does not appear to have been usual in Britain, over the last two decades at least, for the government sector to share anything like fully in economic downturns.[3] This was the case in 1974-75 and 1975-76.

It would seem that the Chancellor was attributing budgetary effects associated with a decline in real economic activity, borne mainly by the private sector, to the effects of inflation *per se*.[4] Contrary to Mr Healey's assertion, it is by no means obvious that the behaviour of the British fiscal system during 1974-75 contradicts the proposition argued in this *Paper* that in general domestically generated inflation *per se* may be expected to generate a proportionate increase in government revenues in excess of the proportionate increase in government expenditures.[5]

---

[1] Budget Statement, *Hansard*, 15 April 1975, column 278.

[2] Clearly it would also have contributed to the rise in government expenditure as increasing numbers received unemployment benefits.

[3] A. R. Prest, 'Sense and Nonsense in Budgetary Policy', *Economic Journal*, March 1968.

[4] It could be argued, of course, that inflation itself caused the decline in economic activity directly. Rapid increases in *real* gross wages probably played an important part in the increase in unemployment. The translation of money into real gross wage increases implies that wage increases were not fully reflected in prices (perhaps because of the price controls). Clearly, it is crucial to distinguish between real gross wage increases and inflation. It may also be argued that the combination of inflation and the tax system contributed directly to the decline in activity. This proposition raises the question whether such a result is due primarily to inflation *per se* or to the unindexed tax system.

[5] A caveat is that the inflation during 1974-75 in part reflected an adverse movement in the terms of trade occasioned by an increase in import prices. This type of inflation does not have the counterpart of increasing domestic incomes that is a feature of domestically generated inflation. Such inflation may increase government expenditure by increasing the prices of goods purchased by the government, or by an obligation to increase transfer payments with the rate of inflation, whatever its source. It was certainly the opinion of the Chancellor that the inflation during 1974-75 was attributable almost exclusively to domestic sources. (*Hansard, op. cit.*, columns 280-282.)

CASH LIMITS—WHAT HAS CHANGED?

Before the 1976-77 Budget, increases in prices and wage-rates during the year were generally met from supplementary provisions. Expenditures appropriated under the Supply Bills required direct Parliamentary consent, but others (for example, where Parliament had simply laid down rules on *how* money was to be spent rather than how *much*) could be approved by Cabinet. In principle, the increases required Treasury scrutiny and Cabinet approval. In practice, they received automatic approval.

The 1976-77 Budget introduced a system of cash limits on expenditure.[1] The limits on central government expenditure are confined mainly to items falling within Supply Bills. Expenditures excluded from limits include National Insurance payments, grants, and subsidies, where expenditure varies in response to the number of beneficiaries. In total, cash limits will be applied to three-quarters of central government voted expenditures other than social security benefits.

Local authority capital expenditures are subject to limits, but not current expenditures. A limit has been placed on the financial assistance grants from the central government. The expenditures of the nationalised industries are excluded, but their estimated financing requirements are to be treated 'as a form of cash limit'.[2] However, it would seem that control is not intended to be rigorous:

> '. . . the limits cannot be immutable because . . . their revenues and expenditures depend on trading conditions. There may well be causes quite beyond the control of a particular industry, reflecting not at all on its efficiency, which would make it exceed its borrowing estimate.'[3]

Cash limits are a statement of good intentions that applies to only a portion of government sector expenditure. The crucial question is what happens when the rate of inflation exceeds that assumed in the initial estimates? The White Paper gives few clues:

> '. . . the Government would have to take stock of the position in the light of all the circumstances of the time.'[4]

This piece of bureaucratese should be clarified by the close of the 1976-77 fiscal year, since the rate of inflation will certainly exceed that indicated in the White Paper, *The Attack on Inflation*, and incorporated in the current expenditure estimates.

---

[1] The detailed methods used and the items to be covered are outlined in the White Paper, *Cash Limits on Public Expenditure*, HMSO, 1976.

[2] *Ibid.,* p. 4.

[3] *Ibid.,* p. 4.

[4] *Ibid.,* p. 5.

QUESTIONS FOR DISCUSSION

1. 'Any attempt to adjust the personal tax system automatically for the effects of inflation would irreparably damage the built-in stability of the economic system.' Discuss.

2. What is the difference, in personal tax equity, between the personal tax increase resulting from 10 per cent inflation and from 10 per cent growth in real income?

3. For wage indexation, it is crucial to distinguish between inflation and changes in *relative* prices in the index used as a basis for adjustment. Does this proposition hold for personal tax indexation?

4. Why does conventional indexation provide inadequate adjustment for the equitable taxation of investment income and capital gains during inflation?

5. 'Indexation limited to personal taxes may increase the inequities arising from inflation.' Criticise.

6. 'Indexation implies a slower rate of growth of the government sector than would otherwise prevail.' Discuss.

7. Can the activity of trade unions mitigate the most adverse effects of the combination of inflation and unchanged personal taxes?

8. 'Indexation would lose the government an important instrument of stabilisation policy.' Do you agree?

9. How does inflation affect the relative contribution of the major taxes to total revenue? To what extent would indexation confined to personal tax alter these consequences?

10. 'Personal tax indexation does not provide governments with more control over the distribution of the personal tax burden. On the contrary, it ties them to a fixed distribution of that burden.' Do you agree?

FURTHER READING

The best general reference is the collection of papers at the 1973 meeting of the International Institute of Public Finance:

Inflation, Economic Growth and Taxation, Institut International de Finances Publiques, Barcelona, 1975.

Allan, J. R., Dodge, D. A., and Podder, S. N., 'Indexing the Personal Income Tax: A Federal Perspective', *Canadian Tax Journal*, July-August 1974.
A description of the Canadian scheme and an excellent discussion of the equity objectives of personal tax indexation.

Petrei, A. H., 'Inflation Adjustment Schemes Under the Personal Income Tax', *International Monetary Fund Staff Papers*, July 1975.
A description of overseas experience with personal tax indexation.

Bossons, J., and Wilson, Thomas A., 'Adjusting Tax Rates for Inflation', *Canadian Tax Journal*, May-June 1973.
Reports on econometric simulations of the effects of indexation on macro-economic stability.

*   *   *

Allen, R. I. G., and Savage, D., 'Inflation and the Personal Income Tax', *National Institute Economic Review*, November 1974; and 'The Case for Inflation-Proofing the Personal Income Tax', *British Tax Review*, No. 5, 1975.

Bacon, Robert, *et al.*, *The Dilemmas of Government Expenditure*, IEA Readings No. 15, Institute of Economic Affairs, London, 1976.

Friedman, Milton, *Monetary Correction*, Occasional Paper 41, Institute of Economic Affairs, London, 1974.

Goetz, Charles L., and Weber, Warren E., 'Intertemporal Changes in Real Federal Income Tax Rates', *National Tax Journal*, March 1971.

Jackman, Richard, and Klappholz, Kurt, *Taming the Tiger*, Hobart Paper 63, Institute of Economic Affairs, London, 1975.

Matthiessen, Lars, 'Index-Tied Income Taxes and Economic Policy', *Swedish Journal of Economics*, March 1973.

OECD, *The Adjustment of Personal Income Tax Systems for Inflation*, OECD, Paris, 1976.

Prest, A. R., 'Inflation and the Public Finances', *Three Banks Review*, March 1973.

Robbins, Lord, *et al.*, *Inflation: Causes, Consequences, Cures*, IEA Readings No. 14, Institute of Economic Affairs, London, 1974 (2nd Impression 1975).

Tanzi, Vito, 'A Proposal for a Dynamically Self-Adjusting Personal Income Tax', *Public Finance*, No. 4, 1966.

SOME IEA PAPERS ON INFLATION, INDEXATION AND TAXATION

INFLATION

Hobart Paperback 4
A Tiger by the Tail
The Keynesian legacy of inflation
F. A. HAYEK
1972   2nd Impression 1973   £1.00
'. . . tantalising excerpts from Hayek's writings, together with a new essay
. . . [which] sets out his thinking with characteristic force . . . In logic
Hayek's proposals make excellent sense.'   Anthony Vice, *The Director*

Occasional Paper 44
Unemployment versus Inflation?
MILTON FRIEDMAN
1975   3rd Impression 1977   £1.00
'. . . perhaps the most important economic pamphlet to be published in
the UK for several decades.'   Samuel Brittan, *Financial Times*

Occasional Paper 47
Catch '76 . . .?
14 Escapes from Economic Derangement
JOHN FLEMMING *et., al.*
1976   £1.50
'For an up-to-date and stimulating view of crisis-strapped Britain this
collection of 14 sharp-shooting essays is highly recommended.'
Sunday Times

Occasional Paper 48
Choice in Currency
A Way to Stop Inflation
F. A. HAYEK
1976   £1.00
'*Choice in Currency* should be regarded, not as a serious proposal, but as a
parable revealing a deeper truth about the nature of inflation.'
Sheffield Morning Telegraph

Readings 14
Inflation: Causes, Consequences, Cures
LORD ROBBINS *et., al.*
1974   2nd Impression 1975   £2.00
'It would be unfair to end this review of a fascinating report without a
mention of Professor Friedman's lucid exposition of the advantages of
voluntary and official indexing as a means of redressing the inequities of
inflation, [and] without a tribute to the brief historical introduction by
Professor Coats that is wise and witty and nicely sceptical . . .'
E. J. Mishan, *The Times Literary Supplement*

[83]

INDEXATION
Hobart Paper 63
Taming The Tiger
RICHARD JACKMAN
KURT KLAPPHOLZ
1975 £1.00
'This debate, at a semi-popular level, should be further advanced by a timely and comprehensive review of the indexation issue published today as an IEA pamphlet.'

Hugh Stephenson, *The Times*

Occasional Paper 41
Monetary Correction
MILTON FRIEDMAN
1974 2nd Impression 1974 60p
'. . . devoted to setting out, with typical verve and vigour, a case for indexation based on a mixture of argument from justice and from expediency. Both categories are extremely interesting and thought provoking . . .'

A. B. Cramp, *Economic Journal*

TAXATION
Hobart Paper 26
Taxmanship
COLIN CLARK
1964 2nd Edition 1970 40p
'Perhaps the most debated question of the day is whether rising wages or rising prices are mainly responsible for inflation.'

Southern Evening Echo

Readings 4
Taxation: A Radical Approach
VITO TANZI, BARRY BRACEWELL-MILNES and D. R. MYDDELTON
1970 90p
'The three essays together illustrate clearly that sharply differential rates, both of direct and indirect taxation, increase the awareness and consequently the "burden" of taxation, and lose revenue. They make a strong case for a shift towards flatter rates of taxation.'

Accountancy

Readings 16
The State of Taxation
A. R. PREST, COLIN CLARK, WALTER ELKAN, CHARLES K. ROWLEY, BARRY BRACEWELL-MILNES, IVOR F. PEARCE.
with an Address by LORD HOUGHTON
1977 Forthcoming

[84]